KCGB: The Boy From the Porch

My Dying Mom and Kurt Cobain

Joseph Hulscher

JPH Publishing LLC

Free, Free, Free at Last

In memory of Mary Jo Hulscher

Table of Contents

Introduction to the Story

~*~

My Dying Mom and Kurt Cobain tell the story of when the world-famous musician came to visit our Mother in the months preceding her death, three years after he took his own life. She knew very little about his legend leading up to her death, not much more than he was from our hometown of Aberdeen, Washington. But her truth was this. She was dying of cancer. It became her mission to figure out who was coming to visit her. Who was this young man with blue eyes? She began to believe it might have been a boy she had helped eleven years ago. The one she was now remembering as, The Boy from the Porch.

They met in the summer of 1986 when he needed a place to stay. He recently spent a week in the Aberdeen City Jail and found himself disconnected from his mother and father. An agreement was made allowing him to sleep in the basement, but this was kept a secret. His visit was brief and insignificant, mostly remembered as just another nameless boy needing help, which is something Mom was known to do, looking out for others.

Mom was diagnosed with Cancer just after the new year in January 1997. It was not good. Terminal lung cancer that had metastasized. Faced with choosing chemo and radiation with all the side effects or seeking alternative medicine as a treatment option, she selected the latter. At the time, Mom and Dad did not share how bad it was with the family. Her body weakened, and she often found herself alone in her room. The month before dying, something or someone pushed her to get out of bed and drive to Seattle, meeting with two of my brothers, asking if either was aware of any interaction our family may have had with the famous music kid from our hometown. Never mentioning him by name, neither brother had any idea whom she was talking about, and oddly enough, neither brother spoke to the other about this until five years later. Hence this remained a mystery. More than a decade after her death, they firmly concluded the boy Mom was talking about was Kurt Cobain.

In a way, this is fortunate for our family. Had we known this story in the years before, it would have been another famous Nirvana story at the height of Kurt's postmortem fame. If we had told the story then, you would have no interest in learning about our Mom. It was easily kept quiet in the family because we had just begun to put the story together. Secondly, in the early years, we would not want our home to be another place for tourists to visit, and many tourists from around the world came to town, still do. The last thing we wanted was people knocking on the front door and inquiring about the private tour of the basement so they could take a picture sitting on that ghetto toilet.

Mom is the driving force behind this memoir. This is the story of her life, the early years growing up, meeting Dad, getting married, starting a family, and her kids' antics. Kurt will play three roles in telling her story, beginning with *Himself* as the world has come to know of him, *The Boy From the Porch*, when he appears in the summer of 1986. and *the Visitor*, as Mom described his presence in 1997. This should help you follow the outline and flow as the author references Kurt Cobain at different points in time when telling this story.

What is a KCGB? It is a particular type of heebie-jeebies courtesy of Frances Bean Cobain, the daughter of Kurt, who inadvertently gives people the K.C. Jeebies for being so similar to her father. The acronym was inspired by Hilly Kristal's CBGB music bar and its impact on the punk scene, and I immediately thought of KCGB for jeebies involving Kurt. I felt some jeebies when writing about his visit with Mom before she died in 1997. Why? Writing about Kurt isn't very comforting; it can be intimidating, almost like sacred ground. Still, it was as if he were saying it was OK to share this story because it would be as if he were advocating for the feminine. Kurt loved his Mom, Wendy, and that is a fact. When his parents split, he longed for a traditional family. He felt that absence when meeting our Mother and other family members.

Five years after Mom died and long after the summer of 1986, my brothers began to put it together, sharing a story that captivated me and everyone involved, bringing my family closer in the years after her passing. In a similar experience, as you read this story, for fans of Kurt, I expect it will bring back your memories of his life, music, death, and the impact all that shit had on you. And to the family and friends of Kurt? I hope it brings you closer, but I doubt you need my help. Now feels like the right time to tell you our story.

KCGB

Act One
My Dying Mom and Kurt Cobain

A Memoir

Joseph Hulscher

Chapter One

"Hey look, there is my Mom,"

Star Date: 1997

"Tim, I think there's someone here to see you."

My brother Tim, known as Old Timer, shared his office at Westin Hotels with his boss and sat with his back to the door, which was why he hadn't seen our mom appear. He was surprised to see her, having never been to his office before, nor had she called ahead. He was also shocked and saddened by her appearance, seeing her many times since being diagnosed with cancer, but this was the first time he thought she looked skinny and worn down. He didn't show it, though, calling out a cheery, "Hey look, there is my Mom," then asked his boss if it was okay to take her to lunch. She had been briefed and knew the situation, agreeing immediately. They made their way to a nearby restaurant in downtown Seattle.

"She sat to my right, Brother Joey," he told me. "Across from me, not directly, but in the seat across from me to the right. We talked about my work and her cancer treatments, telling me she had spent much time in bed lately. We discussed her Starbucks stock. Dad advised her against repurchasing it, but I told her not to listen and to buy back in since she likes it so much. Mom spoke about some church stuff and how she wasn't happy with the feedback she was receiving regarding her chaplain classes. 'You give a lot of power to other people,' I told her. What I meant was she wasn't listening to her gut and letting all these other people tell her what to think.

Then she told me why she had shown up out of the blue. 'Do you remember that duck you drew for the little girl whose daddy died?' she asked me. It took a moment, but then I realized. 'You've always had a deeper connection,' she continued, 'to the spiritual. That's why I can share this with you. Your dad will dismiss it and say it's cancer-playing tricks on my brain. Well, some days I'm half here and half not, and sometimes when I've been like that, someone has been coming to visit me, but I do not know who he is. He's been three times now. He said he has passed on and that I had a big impact on his life.'

My brother listened intently as Mom told him how her visitor was complimentary towards our family, telling her she had done a really good job raising her kids. "He said he interacted with our family, particularly you, Timothy." She remembered three examples, but he could only recall two, once when the visitor said someone in our family had stepped in to stop some kids from hurting him. The other was some connection with our family and a fire involving his brother. "Each time he visits, he shows me things about his life and sometimes private things about me. He took me into the sky, and we hovered over Aberdeen, looking down, showing me where he grew up. Then we moved over to Olympia, and he talked about that. On another visit, we were over Seattle and then over that country that looks like a boot."

"You mean Italy?" — "Yes, that's it."

Our Mom commented, "He says people blame his wife for his death." He wanted her to know his wife hadn't done it and that the drugs clouded his thinking. She received impressions while he told her things and could sense his feelings. The visitor showed her someone described as a law person and the image of a badge, but they weren't a cop or a detective, just someone associated with law enforcement. They were making life hard for his wife and causing his family much pain and grief. "Timothy, you remember helping a kid about ten years ago, letting him stay at our house? That boy from the porch?"

"Vaguely," Old Timer replied.

"It's that boy who is coming to visit me. I think he was part of that band." — "What band?" — "That famous one from Aberdeen. Do you know anyone who was in that band?" — "I think you mean Nirvana. No, I don't think I knew any of them."

Mom went on, "He was brought into the world to give people hope and was born to influence millions. There's enough pain and suffering in the world, and he felt bad about it, pausing as if unable to find the words when finishing, for killing himself."

They continued discussing various things, but nothing helped Old Timer understand what Mom wanted him to learn. At one point, suggesting the visitor was maybe referring to someone else. This frustrated Mom, "Do you even believe me? Do I sound crazy? Do you remember the boy we helped?" My brother did not recall anything but told her, "I'm sure what you're telling me isn't a waste of time. Maybe it's not meant for now and will be important information in the future." He returned to his office, having made a mental note that this was out of the ordinary for Mom, something very unusual, thinking it would mean something to him in the future. His boss inquired, but he declined to discuss it.

~*~

Old Timer later told me, "There have been numerous occasions where something has happened. Instead of having a deja-vu feeling, I had the opposite – anticipation of deja-vu happening in the future. As strong as deja-vu but the opposite." About five years later, this made sense when he visited a music store that was going out of business, stocking up on loads of old CDs. Simon & Garfunkel, John Denver, Scorpions, REO Speedwagon, Fleetwood Mac, and Nirvana. When he got into the Nirvana CD, he researched the band online and ran into all the history and conspiracy theories. Shortly afterward, his conversation with Mom came back to him. It was a spine-tingling Holy Shit moment.

I wasn't surprised that Mom reached out to the wise one of her six children that day. Our brother Tim is the old soul with whom she'd had many discussions on new age matters. And it's not uncommon for people near the end of their life to have visits from a loved one who has preceded them in death. Mom had learned this from her books and discussions with him and the patients at the hospital she visited as a chaplain.

In 1997 Mom's body was losing its fight with lung cancer, yet she refused to consider chemotherapy or radiation. There was an understanding that while the chemicals may prolong her life, they could also harm the healthy cells and bring terrible side effects. She chose Gerson Therapy because of her unwavering belief in holistic medicine as the right approach to achieve a miraculous recovery from terminal cancer. This approach limited calorie intake to only fresh organic fruits and vegetables compressed into liquid form via a juicer we had set up in the kitchen. She was also prescribed vitamin supplements and frequent enemas, failing to give her the results she expected, let alone needed three months removed from her initial diagnosis.

After her chat with Old Timer, Mom returned to her car and headed south on I-5 and thru the ever-present construction around the Tacoma Dome. A flood of memories returned when passing the exit she took if going to her childhood home in the Proctor District and then the 56th Street and S. Oakes exit, where her in-laws lived, before making it through the interstate bottleneck that leads into the Nisqually Valley. She hoped to get to our cabin in Columbus Park on Black Lake, leaving time for a nap before meeting with the next son on this journey.

She found comfort near Black Lake, where our family had spent countless summer hours. Dad bunked there when he started working in Chehalis after the local hospital closed in our hometown of Aberdeen. He returned to school and earned a master's in health administration, hoping a new position might grant him a shorter commute. Many of us crashed at the cabin at different points in our lives. It was a place you were always welcome to party at the lake.

Seeing the mailboxes on the right, Mom knew to turn left into Columbus Park. From there, she drove past the guard shack, where a day visitor stopped to pay the entrance fee and saw the lake when hitting the top of the hill. Black Lake drains into the Chehalis River, Grays Harbor, and the Pacific Ocean. There was a right at the bottom and a small bridge crossing Scott Creek, where salmon once returned from the ocean to spawn, the creek that ran along the reserved campsites. The gravel road turned to the right until she instinctively turned left into a track that led to a giant boulder at the end. Our cabin was to the left of the boulder. The Sleepy Hollow sign above the front door was a welcome sight, having repurposed it from her summer camp years as a counselor so it could hang on ours. It felt like home.

She met with my brother John, known to most people as Spud. He lived at the cabin more often than the rest of us. Mom described her visitor as a young man who wanted to compliment our family and added a description that must have been specifically for him, asking John about a fire. He did not remember anything that could help until she brought up her interest in the music kid, the one from the famous band from our hometown, the one who died. He had a pretty good idea who Mom was talking about. Anyone who grew up near Grays Harbor and Aberdeen would know who she was talking about. But like my brother Old Timer, Spud had no memory of meeting Kurt Cobain.

After their chat, Mom headed for home, an hour away, without getting her questions answered. Neither brother knew who *this visitor* was or how we knew him. She found comfort in talking with the Old Timer, though. Thinking of their conversation as her Honda Accord made its way through the Black Hills, Mom wanted to be clear when she told them, "What I am experiencing is very real to me." My brothers assured her, "You are not crazy, Mom."

~*~

Old Timer told me one of their earliest conversations about spiritual stuff was in the first or second grade. They sat together at the dining table and talked about his quiet and shy personality. He mentioned to Mom that he'd had experiences that made him think he might have a connection to the spiritual, giving one example he doesn't recall and a second involving Christina Pierce, his classmate, whose father had died unexpectedly.

— She was out of class for a few days, Joey, so the teacher had us write personal notes to her to tell her how sorry we all were. The teacher sent the notes to her house so she knew everyone was thinking about her. I was just a little kid and didn't know what to write, so after sitting there for a while, I decided to draw a picture instead. I contemplated and then ended up drawing a duck. It was one of my more realistic, colorful drawings, and I felt good about it. It was a small duck, flat on the bottom as if sitting in water. I never wrote anything except my name—just the picture. And I was a bit worried because I hadn't written anything, and a duck had nothing to do with the situation. When Christina finally returned to class, she wanted to discuss my card. She pulled me aside and asked, 'How did you know?' I didn't know what she meant, and she asked why I didn't write anything but just drew a picture. I told her I didn't know what to write, so I wanted to draw a picture and hoped that was okay. She started to cry and explained that my card was her favorite and that her dad loved to duck hunt. He went all the time. Ducks were a big part of his life. She wondered how I could have known to draw a duck like that. It was very personal to her and to me. —

Hearing this for the first time, I was blown away. In our youth, my siblings and I did not fully understand this concerning our brother Tim, and we just knew that he acted like he had an old soul and that his view of the world differed from ours. This is another reinforcement of why we call him Old Timer.

Growing up, my brother was really into Star Trek, the Twilight Zone, the Night Stalker, and all kinds of paranormal stuff. Leonard Nimoy, who played Spock in Star Trek, hosted a program called "In Search Of," with stories like Big Foot, UFOs, the Loch Ness Monster, reincarnation, ghosts, and whatnot. Watching that led Old Timer to read many books on those subjects. Mom knew he liked exploring these issues but disapproved when he purchased one book in particular – Hal Lindsey's The Late Great Planet Earth, about the Antichrist, the rapture, the sign of the beast, Armageddon, how Russia was going to be the bad guy and the Antichrist will come out of the so-called United States of Europe. Old Timer shared each chapter's pronouncements with Mom, keeping her updated and expounding on any wacky thing that it might be saying. She would listen. Kind of.

Later he became curious about life after death and discovered James Van Praagh, a medium and clairvoyant. When Old Timer shared his stories about near-death experiences, she began talking to him about Shirley MacLaine, who was exploring and writing about new-age spirituality then. MacLaine was a heroine of hers. Mine too. Mom spoke about Edgar Cayce, known as The Sleeping Prophet, who cured people with advice from a trance state and made numerous predictions, not unlike Nostradamus.

Another book he read and shared was "The Holy Blood and The Holy Grail" by Michael Baigent, Richard Leigh, and Henry Lincoln. The book examined the theory that Jesus was married to Mary Magdalene and had children before sneaking them away to Southern France before his death on the cross. It states that the Holy Grail refers to the holy bloodline that has continued since Jesus married and fathered a child. Mom thought that was blasphemy, but it eventually became a big deal in her life and was the main reason she wanted to go to France and see the black Madonna statues and paintings and some of the places mentioned in the book.

Mom eventually got brave enough to see a medium for at least one session, which was recorded and played for us kids. The medium said one thing about Old Timer, then a ton of stuff about his identical twin, Terry, and some about the rest of the family. Mom apologized when the medium had little about him, as she knew it meant a great deal based on their similar interests and conversations.

The recording was shared with me. I took it to my 1973 VW Super-Beetle and popped it into the cassette deck to listen. I returned to the house just as much of a skeptic as I was before. The medium said there would be a baby and the State of Oregon would play an essential role in my future. I told Mom I wasn't about to have a baby as I was going to university, nor did I intend to live in or move to Oregon. Spirit was right on this one. Within three years, I would accept a transfer to Bend, Oregon, and another three years after, Mom became a grandmother when Heather was born in Salem, Oregon.

I gathered there is no statute of limitations regarding mediums, meaning the message you receive now may only have understanding later. That's how it worked out for Old Timer and the lunch conversation with Mom, and that is the way it worked out for Me and the State of Oregon. I have long since become a believer in the connection to the spiritual. My brother Old Timer and his little duck understood this long before the rest of us.

Chapter Two

The Early Years

Star Date: 1935-1960

Mom and her sister Patty

~*~

Arriving in a small body weighing just over three pounds, Mom was born in August 1935 at St Joseph Hospital in Tacoma, Washington. At such a size, she had to be a fighter and had true grit from the minute she arrived until the moment of her death. Her mom, Helen Francis Reed, worked full-time as a telephone switchboard operator with the Pacific Bell Telephone Company until retirement. Working full-time was not her choice – her husband was an alcoholic. Priests and other folk had advised Mrs. Reed to leave the marriage, but she stuck it out until her husband died in February of 1973. Helen only spoke of being with one other person in her lifetime. She'd had a boyfriend from Wisconsin who went away to war and never came back. It must have been quite a loss at such a young age.

Granny, as we called her, was wonderful with her grandchildren, taking turns sitting on her lap and reading us books such as "Fawn Baby" by Gladys Baker Bond. You could always find one of those big containers of Apricot Nectar in her ice box – the ones for which you used a triangle can-opener to pop two holes in the top. Without a car, the resourceful Mrs. Reed took the bus to the mall to buy us presents for Christmas and would always send a card or letter for our birthdays. Rarely did she miss honoring a birthday or graduation. The only time I remember her being cross was when I went off upstairs alone and rummaged through an old trunk. I was searching for treasure, and as I made my way downstairs waving a flag and carrying my newfound booty, she caught me as I reached the bottom and turned me right around. She sternly suggested I put things back where I found them and asked that I never get into her things again, with a single swat on the butt for motivation.

Helen about 1914 or 1916

Joseph Reed lied about his age and joined the Merchant Marines to escape a father who sometimes beat him. Mom's father sailed the ocean blue and traveled to many parts of the world, never holding down a professional line of work. Later in life, he excelled as a prolific letter writer, offering his opinions to the local newspaper. A factor that complicated his life was his alcoholic binges that did not subside for days and weeks. We never had much interaction with Papa Joe before he died. None of us can recall him playing with his grandchildren. My father, Pops, says he mostly sat in his chair, reading the newspaper, smoking, and watching the television. Mom did not have fond memories of her father when he was a heavy drinker. In almost every picture I could find, he can be seen holding a lit cigarette, which she was required to fetch from the store, which was common back in the day. His breath would smell of tobacco and alcohol, finding it disgusting when in this state of intoxication, he would become affectionate and kiss her. The only time he was affectionate was when he was drinking. His binges could go on for months, followed by sobriety and another binge that would not subside until he ended up in the hospital or the drunk tank. In the end years, he found peace from his demons tending to the flowers and rose bushes in their modest yard when not writing letters to the editor, humorously replying to himself using the pseudonym of one of his grandchildren.

Papa Joe Merchant Marines

With Granny working hard in their early years, Mom and her sister Patty, two years younger, were cared for by others. Mom's first recollection of a nanny was Ana, but then one day, when she was three or four years old, her mother said that Ana was gone with little or no explanation. This was hard for her to comprehend, and it hurt deeply. There would be a few other women who cared for the young girls as they grew older but no more nannies. Eventually, Mom was made to take responsibility for herself and her sister until their mother came home from work. From early childhood, she was on her own much of the time. Her sister Aunty Pat shared that Mom spent much time alone upstairs while Aunty would hang out in the kitchen with Granny and talk about stuff while they made dinner.

The sisters attended Saint Patrick grade school and Aquinas Academy, which the Sisters of Saint Dominic founded in 1893. St Thomas Aquinas Academy was the area's first Catholic Girls' high school, operating at the turn of the century. At ages 13 and 14, Mom attended Marylac summer camp, owned and operated by the Dominican Sisters. She was a reporter for the NW Progress, a regional Catholic newspaper, and in the early 50s, attended the first two Catholic Youth Organization summer camps. These were developed by Father Richard Stohr, who became a lifelong friend. Mom was initially hired as a camp counselor and assistant lifeguard. But her swimming was so superior to the lifeguard's that it wasn't long before she took over the role, along with all the responsibilities of the supervision and safety of the swimmers.

Father Stohr was a big tease and slept in the attic of the chapel. Mom wanted to get even with him one morning, so she set the alarm and got up at about 4 am. She must have smiled in anticipation as her little feet moved quickly towards the chapel and the rope leading up to the attic, which connected to the bells that would ring close to Father Stohr's sleeping. With juvenile excitement and delight, she gave that rope a couple of powerful pulls, letting the chapel bells ring loud and proud, to her heart's delight. But there was a problem with her prank. In addition to startling Father Stohr, she woke everyone else, including the cook, who was not the least happy. She was on kitchen duty for the remainder of the day, but I expect she peeled potatoes with a sheepish grin and quiet giggles, maybe planning her next shenanigan.

Despite a string-bean build and a weight of 100 lbs, Mom was athletic and played basketball and tennis while in school. Besides the water, tennis was her love, and she continued to play until her child-rearing responsibilities took over. Mom so loved her church that following graduation from high school in 1953, she entered the convent with the Dominican Sisters. Why she would join the convent was beyond me, and Aunty Pat could not explain. I wondered if she thought every day would be like summer camp or that maybe she'd wanted to get away from her father, and I believed it was a path she did not fully understand.

I mentioned this to Dad, who said this wasn't the case. "Your Mom was fully aware and had been influenced by 12 years of Catholic schooling by sisters and was greatly influenced by nuns and priests; both had become substitutes for parental figures." Pops wasn't done, "Joseph, unless you are a person of great faith, you may not understand; your mother had such a strong belief in promoting the church's work that she wanted to be part of it and felt a need to work in it. She always maintained this calling towards her ministry." Either way, (I love my Dad), the truth was a rigid and repressive environment was prevalent in the church's religious orders at the time. The order of the day included taking vows of poverty, chastity, and obedience. This was the choice our mother made. The Catholic faith recognizes that taking on a new name is symbolic of entering into a new place in one's life in the religious, so Mom took on the name Sister Mary Xavier.

Aunty Pat and Sister Mary Xavier

In those days, the new sisters taught school with only a high school diploma, so Sister Mary Xavier taught grade school in Yakima at St Paul's and in Seattle at St Joseph's. According to Aunty Pat, who kept in touch with her sister, "Life was pretty stern in the convent." She was forced to play the organ for events and gatherings, and even as a schoolteacher, she had a particular lights-out time. I imagine it went like this, starting with a knock on the door with instructions to turn out the lights. "May I have more time to grade papers, Mother Superior?" Only to see a ruler the size of a yardstick appear and flip the light switch down. Aunty Pat shared, "But that did not stop your mom; after the door closed, she pulled the covers over her head to block the light from her flashlight as she graded papers under cover of darkness." This would not be Mom's first or last conflict with her church.

Dad told me that by 1958 Sister Mary Xavier "could no longer reconcile herself to the permanent vows in the order of sisterhood and chose to pursue her vocations as a lay person." Knowing Mom, this was not an easy decision to make, but in the end, it was time to get on with living when she chose to leave the convent. Mom must have taken a massive breath of fresh air when she stepped out of the rigid confines of the Dominican Sisters and into the brave new world – albeit one where you had to obtain a liquor permit to purchase alcohol, which she did on Tuesday, November 25th, 1958. Most likely, it was a bottle of wine to share with her sister when celebrating Thanksgiving just a few days later.

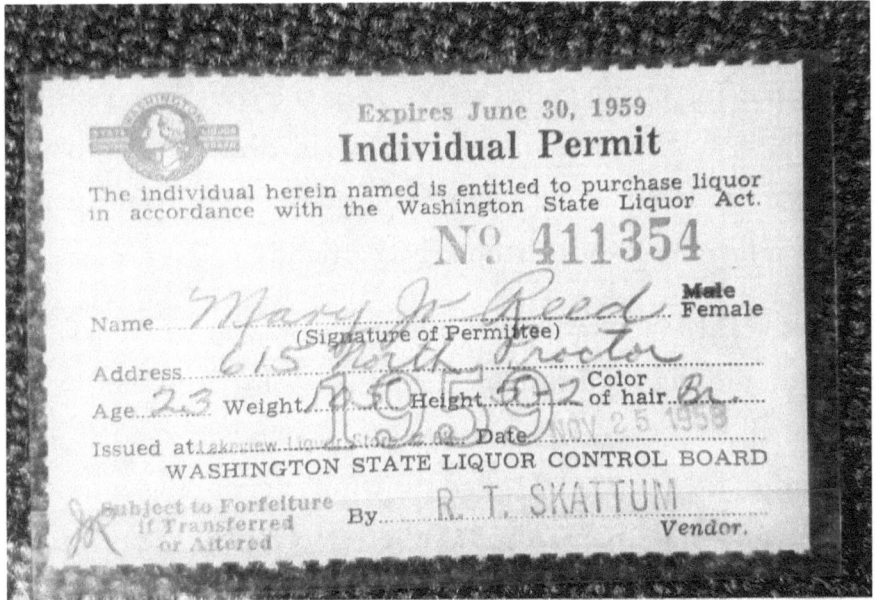

Mom went to work for the state of Washington in the personnel office, becoming a legislative aide to the Democratic Party and private secretary to the Pierce County Sheriff. She also attended the young adult church group called Cardinal Club and reunited with her sister Patty, who had a head start on the social scene after graduating from Aquinas. Aunty Pat entered the dating pool and soon after married Uncle Bob and immediately started a family, as good Catholics did back in the day. To us, that would mean four cousins to play with when Mom visited Patty in Tacoma, two blocks from Granny's, and later when her sister moved to beautiful Missoula, Montana, and the home of the Grizzlies. Mom had a pretty good cry in 1973 when Aunty Pat tiptoed around the news before finding courage and telling her sister, "We're moving."

The Cardinal Club was a good business plan for the church. The sooner young adults get married, the sooner they will put kids into the system. More kids in the system meant more butts in the pews, and more butts in the pews would keep the church coffers full. Let the cash register ring. Soon after, two love birds began to have googly eyes for each other. Mom and Dad were a perfect match as both came from devout Catholic backgrounds.

Dad was raised in a Catholic family with a socially drinking father and a disciplinarian Mother. His father, John Hulscher, was a jack of all trades when working with his hands. Grandad John was just called Grandad. He had the strongest hands, giant meaty palms, and a smile that made everyone feel special. Grandad was the best. He was always helping with construction around the house, putting on roofs, patching a chimney, and even digging out the basement of the Oakes Street home by hand – one wheelbarrow at a time, according to Dad. His brother Bert, father to cousin Bernie, gets credit for using the term Camel Time. It was eleven in the morning on the dirt project when Bert asked, "What does it take to get a drink around here? What do you think I am, a camel?" Raise your glass, bourbon on the rocks with a splash – it is never too early for camel time. Construction projects and camel time became family traditions. Thank you, Uncle Bert.

I started calling Grandad "Jake," like I heard my dad call him once. But if I did so, he would reach out to shake my hand, grab it, put his other hand on top, and squeeze hard. He would combine this vice-like grip with a laugh, a twinkle in his eye, and call me Alec. Not because it was my name but because I was a Smart Alec. Dad told me I should not call him Jake as it was a term of endearment between them. I discovered that one of Grandad's brothers called him Jake the Flake while digging out the basement. So, I never called him Jake when Dad was around. It was something special kept between Grandad and me.

Grandad in the middle with a Coca-Cola

Hulscher is a unique name that has been traced back to Holland. For fun, you should google Heineken and Hulscher, and you will learn of two Hulscher Brothers who were part of the beer establishment and the Hotel Die Port van Cleve in Amsterdam.

Dad's mom Violet is a descendant of the Scrutons of South Dakota. Scruton Mountain was named after two brothers who operated a gold mine at the base of the mountain during the early years of the

Black Hills gold rush. These brothers managed to keep the location of the mine secret. When the last brother died, the mystery of the site died with him. Later, President Theodore Roosevelt initiated action to change the mountain's name to Bullock Peak. Since then, the mountain has worn two labels: Scruton Mountain and Seth Bullock Lookout.

Violet was born in Lead, South Dakota, close to the former lawless and rowdy town of Deadwood, made famous in the HBO series. Her mother was born in Pennington, South Dakota, and lived in a cabin on Mount Rushmore, playing on the mountain before the carving began. The Lakota called this granite formation Tunkasila Sakpe Paha, or Six Grandfathers Mountain before a land dispute resulted in a name change, a polite way of saying their land was stolen despite an 1868 treaty granting exclusive use to the Sioux.

Compared to Grandad John, Grandma Violet was the stern disciplinarian in the family growing up. If Dad were to run off at the mouth or slip up in a way that did not meet her standards, she would crack open dried hot peppers on his tongue. I remember Mom handling things differently when I must have said something of similar vulgarity. No peppers for me; instead, I was marched into the bathroom, where she stuffed my head in the toilet and flushed it, telling me, "Talk like that belongs in the sewer." I cried as she comforted me while helping me dry my hair. So, while I got a swirly and a towel from my mom, Dad could have used a glass of milk. Don't get me wrong, Grandma Violet was very good with the grandkids and took ownership of the kitchen. She would bake a spread of cookies for holidays, and Grandad would offer the boys a drink when they were of proper age. Proper, according to him. It was camel time at Grandad's on holiday, and he was good for a drink and a smile. They were both excellent hosts.

There were four children in my dad's family. The oldest sibling John, known as Jack, entered the priesthood, and we came to know him as Father Alfred. With a priest in the tribe, we had the golden ticket to heaven.

Jack (Fr. Alfred) holding unknown
toddler, Dad, Louise

Alfred liked to sit us kids on his lap and then make the sound of a buzzing bee until he pinched you. You would run away, and the next kid in line would get stung. Dad came next in birth, followed by his sister Louise, who married Uncle Dick and gave us seven cousins to play with. Good Catholics. Much later, Richard, known as Uncle Zag arrived and was more like a big brother than an uncle to us as the years passed.

Dad graduated from Bellarmine Prep and earned a college degree from St Martin's. He started going to Cardinal Club events, where he caught the eye of Mom. In her wedding book, she wrote that "he seemed shy until mistletoe time came around," and then they started to notice each other more and more at different functions. Dad said he was a bit slow on the uptake, commenting, "It was only when Mary Jo asked me if I knew of any other boys that I took the hint!" They went on their first date on December 12, 1959, and were engaged officially on March 1, 1960. It was announced in the Tacoma News Tribune on April 17, 1960. Mom said they stayed out until 5 am and waited until they could see the picture in the paper. The love birds were married on July 9, 1960, in a huge Catholic wedding – the first officiated by the newly ordained minister of the cloth, Father Alfred (Jack). It was a great day, and when it was over, Mom and Dad set out down the Oregon Coast for their honeymoon.

The day before the wedding, Mom and Dad agreed it would be best if he chose six months of active duty in the National Guard with a deferred entry to avoid the potential of a future draft. In those days when your number was up, it required mandatory enlistment into national service. And with the decision made, in October of 1960, Dad left for Fort Ord, leaving Mom home alone. When returning west for Christmas leave, Mom cornered him, "Enough is enough."

"Screw this, Ronnie, I'm coming with you," although the exact terminology is unknown, there would be no more playing home alone, and east they went. Dad had been transferred to Aberdeen, Maryland, so they lived there until active duty was completed in April of 1961. Free to travel, they took the southern route home and visited the Grand Canyon and relatives in Vegas and Compton. They intended to live in Tacoma, but Dad found work in Aberdeen, Washington.

They lived in an apartment and later rented a house before purchasing their first home on I Street. They were delighted with their home, within walking distance of the Catholic church and school. Dad went to work at the Weyerhaeuser Company at the Cosmopolis office and, as a keen golfer, may have been in heaven when he learned this was just below the local Golf Course, Highland GC. He won the company golf tournament in 1962. Dad also worked for Rayonier before finding permanent work at St Joseph Hospital, an occupation where he would learn the ins and outs of hospital fiscal management and rural hospital administration. He excelled at this area of expertise throughout his remaining work years.

Mom also went to work for Weyerhaeuser the first summer and got a job at the Aberdeen Federal Savings and Loan Bank before becoming the full-time YMCA director for her soon-to-be-born four boys. The newlyweds were well on their way, and the 60s were coming into full bloom, and they owned a home and were looking forward to the future and starting a family.

Chapter Three

A Lovely Young Man

Star Date: May 1997

The Sound of Silence by Simon and Garfunkel is playing in the background. We are in Mom's bedroom, and she is nearing the end of her life with only a few months to live. She was alone and in darkness when an old friend called upon her. *This is the first of his four visits and is a dramatized visualization based on the events described in the weeks preceding her death.*

The first time the visitor came to see Mom, he had nothing to say, never speaking. She briefly went in and out of sleep when realizing someone was sitting across the room. Beside her on the nightstand was her book, a glass of carrot juice, and, crucially, her glasses, which meant there was only a fuzzy outline of an image. She nodded for a second, and then something got her attention; the same someone was now standing, and it was as if they were admiring the furniture in her room, then walking about and touching each piece. These were a matched set of mid-century traditional, cherry mahogany elegance that gave our mother pride even after all these years. It was her original and only bedroom set. As she gathered herself, it could be determined the silhouette was that of a young man with a slender outline.

He walked over, pulled up the corner of a huge rug that would take hundreds of dollars to clean, and then looked around at the built-in closets an artisan must have made in the early 1900s. He said nothing, just wandered. It was as if he were doing the same as her, like when you wake up and try to get your bearings because you are unsure of where you are. He checked his heart and hands as if taking an inventory upon his arrival like you might if you had just appeared – teleporting in from the other side.

Heaven assumed Mom thought in reverse deja-vu as they looked out the window onto the Chehalis River and Grays Harbor. She had no idea what that phrase could mean, but it sounded lyrical and fit the mystery of his presence. Yet there he was, standing shoulders high in her room. Was he sent from heaven, or was she coining a phrase and just another time when Mom gave meaning to something for someone to understand later? Life creates a perfect circle sometimes in that way. Most likely, it was her head getting misty, like when the fog rolled in with the river at the very end of the day. Just as she asked herself where he had come from, she found herself asking where he had gone. Was he not just standing over there? Perhaps Mom was lucid dreaming in the sleep phase of rapid eye movement, the stage in which most dreams occur.

In truth, his visit brought comfort to Mom. She enjoyed occasionally having someone in her room, particularly those already in the know, never to bring up her cancer. This was key and make no mistake. Mom had a rule. Anyone visiting was instructed to avoid discussing her health situation or expressing sympathy. There would be none of that, and as one visitor found out, she outright asked them to leave. There was another time when she asked Dad to come into her room, sharing her true feelings in private, telling him who it was that she wished never to see again, and he took care of it in the way and manner he always did, with dignity and grace. It was nice this visitor had taken the time to see her as others had stayed away, finding strength when her children and those within her inner circle came to check in on her. Like them, he understood the rules and never spoke of death. There was something in the way he carried himself, definitely something in the way. What a lovely young man.

Mom - Sedona, Arizona.

Chapter Four

Life in the '60s

Star Date 1961 - 1973

By the end of August 1961, Mom would have known she was pregnant. The young couple was excited while waiting for their first child's birth. The following spring, the contractions started, and they went to the hospital a few blocks away. And on March 29, 1962, a son was welcomed into the world. The following is from a brief letter Dad sent his children about our brother John Joseph.

— It was March 29, 1962, when your brother John Joseph was born. He was named after his grandfathers, John on the paternal side and Joseph on the maternal side. Your mom had a very short labor, as she did with all of her babies. Your mother was a trooper. In 1962, fathers were not allowed in the delivery room or to hold the baby after he was born. The baby remained in the hospital until it went home. The father could not be present in a room with the baby. When labor kicked in, I went to the father's waiting room. I did not see your mom until she returned to her hospital room. The baby was in the nursery. When I walked into the room, she was sitting up in bed. Her face was radiant and the happiest I had ever seen her. As far as we knew, the baby was just fine. I was never allowed to hold your brother John Joseph.

In those days, the standard time for mothers in the hospital was three days. Fathers went home after the birth and only visited twice a day. The baby spent time with its mother, and I was dispatched home after he was born. I checked in with your mom a couple of times each day. The baby started to develop a jaundice condition when the skin coloring turned yellow. Jaundice occurs when the liver converts red blood cells into new ones the body cannot eliminate. The yellow is bilirubin.

In 1962, one remedy was to do a total blood transfusion in which they replaced the baby's blood. Dr. Fulton exchanged John Joseph's blood, and Mom was sent home when, later that day, the hospital called to say that John Joseph had died. He had lived three and a half days. One of the sisters baptized him. We were unprepared for that result and planned to move to Tacoma. John Joseph is buried in the Little Angels section at Calvary Cemetery in South Tacoma. I wanted you to know the story of your oldest brother. He resembled my Father and Spud.

Love, Dad —

John Joseph died due to rh incompatibility. The baby was rh positive born to an rh negative mother. Infants with mild rh incompatibility may be treated with phototherapy using bilirubin lights or IV immune globulin. An exchange transfusion of blood may be needed for severely affected infants. Our sister is rh negative, they gave her a shot first trimester, and that was that. In other words, if John Joseph had been born today, he most likely would be alive. This was undoubtedly the lowest point in our parent's life.

The death of John Joseph was devastating. The God they respected and worshipped was not making it easy for them. Some say the *Heavenly Father* does not give you more than you can handle, and it was not long after when they realized this, and Mom became pregnant again. Throughout the pregnancy, one could expect there was worry about the baby's health, and sure enough, just after the birth in May 1963, the doctor asked my parents which they wanted to know first, the good news or the bad news. That took a breath away as they waited for what came next.

The good news was the baby boy was healthy. The bad news was that he had a condition called clubfoot and would need to wear shoe braces for a year to straighten his feet out. Clubfoot, also called talipes, is where one or both feet are rotated inward and downward. So, it was the oldest — James Ronald who became the Forrest Gump of our family. His awkward gait resulted in his classmates at school teasing him relentlessly and saying he ran funny, like a turkey. On the last day of school before Thanksgiving break, he was chased thru Sam Benn Park on his way home, making it to safety before anything happened, creating the legend of Turk, short for Turkey. We still refer to him as Brother Turk, as do many of his childhood friends.

In February 1965, — Joseph Patrick, your guide, was born. I am known to the family as Brother Joey. My friends call me a lot of other things. According to Dad, the doctors had concerns about rh or something else, so Mom was advised, "No breastfeeding." I was put on the bottle. This might be something for my therapist to consider. Looking at my baby pictures, I'm surprised I was never confused with the family pig. I was a porker. Dad says my protein-based formula was adjusted accordingly, and as my mobility and metabolism improved, overeating never resulted in a weight problem.

Eighteen months later, in August 1966, the baby-making newlyweds were blessed with twins. — Timothy Gerard (Old Timer) arrives first, followed a few minutes later by — Terence Dominic (Balboa). And just like that, by the end of summer 1966, Mom and Dad had gone from losing a child only four years earlier to a tribe of four little hoodlums. It was time for the stork to take a vacation. For a few years, there was a break in the action.

Joey, Balboa, Old Timer, Turk in December 1967

While the stork took a vacation from our household, Donald and Wendy Cobain received two visits. In February of 1967, they welcomed a baby boy to their family and named the cute fellow — Kurt Donald. He was described as happy and energetic, with a strong interest in music, beginning to sing along to songs at age two and playing piano at age 4. In 1969 the family moved into the now-historic 1210 E. First St. home. His sister — Kimberley Dawn, was born in April of 1970, and for a few years, they experienced the ideal family dynamic as playful siblings.

Back in our home, Mom found herself grateful that the good Lord had given her a healthy family but faced the oldest boy of three years and three months, an eighteenth-month wild boar of a son, and newborn twins. The rocking chair and changing table would be busy. With a growing family, it was time to upgrade, and it was heaven for us boys when we moved to the house on McKinley across from Sam Benn Park. Who needs a yard when you have an entire park to explore with creeks, salamanders, large trees to climb, trails to follow, a playground turned sandlot, neighbor kids, and occasional hippies who hung out, smoked doobies, and played guitar? It looked nothing like it does today.

The stork returned from vacation and, in February 1970, delivered — John Daniel. Kind and sensitive, through the years, we called him Johnny and, later, Brother Spud. Meanwhile, our Mom was having a pressing conversation with God after going 0-6 in an effort toward bringing a girl into this world. You can bet these were serious discussions because the Big Kahuna was listening, and in March of 1973, Mom did give birth to a baby girl—this more than filled her heart with great joy, so much so that she named her little bundle — Maria Joy. Admiring the Harper Lee book "To Kill a Mockingbird" and the character of Scout so much that she added it along to her name. So now we had a beautiful sister named Maria Joy Scout. My cousins remember how happy their Aunt Jo (Mom) was with the arrival of her daughter. Dad was handing out cigars.

With six kids in tow, the park across the street became Mom's haven as much as ours. We explored every inch of it in the years we lived in the McKinley house. Back then, the park was the entire world to us, and we would go as far as we wanted as long as it was within the boundaries of that park. Those were some memorable days for us; we were some kooky kids. We would be gone for hours and only come home for a meal or a snack. This brought a little peace until we all came home needing a bath and a complete change of clothes. The mess hall and laundry room must have run 24 hours a day.

Our house on McKinley was getting a little small with six kids, two adults, and Agnes, the cat. We would need a bigger boat to coin the phrase from Jaws. And Dad did that by finding one of those big houses built early in the Broadway Expansion years. Before 1903 there were a dozen or more homes above 8th and Broadway, but 46 or more magnificent homes were built in this area in the ten years that followed. The pace slowed during the First World War and peaked with 53 homes built between 1920 and the stock market crash of 1929. This was Aberdeen at its finest, earning the title of Lumber Capital of the World. * Build records estimated using current tax records of existing homes.

So, one day, Dad said we were moving, and we were going to take a look at our new house six blocks away. We piled into the wagon, and away we went. The place, which I nicknamed Pilgrim Heights, was huge, with steps at the front and two tall pillars. We immediately started jumping off the bulkheads and onto the grass below, a five-foot drop from which we landed and rolled down a small hill. Then we ran through the house and up the stairs. It was a converted duplex with eight bedrooms and two sets of stairs. We could go up either side. Some bolted left, and some went right.

Mom and Dad had already picked out their room with its light yellowing wallpaper. Each bedroom was papered a different color. It was easy for Joy Scout to be assigned a room, as one was pink. Turk chose the orange room, Balboa the red room, I selected the blue room, and Spud and Old Timer took rooms dead center in the house that were separated by two doors that rolled shut and could be locked with a bit or barrel key. Later I traded with Old Timer to hang out closer with Spud and eventually took over the pink room after painting it blue and gold. One of the upstairs rooms that could have been another bedroom became the TV room with an old couch and chair. It was also our playroom.

We were enthusiastic and excited due to the size of this place, but I felt a loss being away from the park. Since we had Sam Benn, we'd never really used our previous yard, but at Pilgrim Heights, we converted the backyard into our sports mecca, starting with a baseball field. Grandad helped put a basketball hoop on the garage roof, and we played football in the street or the area in front of Benn Gym. Next, we made a golf course with one hole in the ground and nine different locations to start from. Pops initiated safety lessons after Old Timer accidentally conked the neighbor kid in the head during a practice swing, requiring stitches. Note — Dave Grohl shared in his recent memoir *The Storyteller* of searching for his mom Virginia with his head matted with blood after being crowned with a golf club by another child. Some things in life are universal. Pops substituted plastic golf balls after I broke a window with a real golf ball.

I don't recall being told when moving day was upon us. I came home from school – the McKinley house was being emptied, and Dad said we're leaving today and will be at Pilgrim Heights this evening. It was good that Dad knew what was going on when I saw a bag of candy on the counter, and I asked if I could have a piece. "Yes," he said. The candy impacted my memories more than the moving van with the Mayflower ship parked outside.

Chapter Five

I Wanted to Thank You

Star Date: May 1997

Mrs. Robinson by Simon and Garfunkel plays in the background. We've returned to Mom's bedroom. She is nearing the end of her life with only a few months to live. This is the second of four visits and is a dramatized visualization based on the events she described in the weeks preceding her death.

Mom fumbled for her pointy framed glasses with lenses the size of Coke bottles shaped like cat eyes, patting the bedspread until she remembered they were on the nightstand. Her vision became focused as she looked around the room and saw that he was back.

Seeing more than just the fuzzy outline of his image, she sized him up. *Hmm,* thinking as she stretched, but for her life, she did not recognize her visitor. He was sitting comfortably in the rocking chair, leaning back with his legs stretched out and crossed at the ankle. He wore an olive-colored cardigan sweater with a button-up shirt over a white t-shirt. She noticed he was wearing a watch on his left wrist, and his jeans were ripped around the left knee.

She thought they could be mended with a patch as done on her boys' Toughskin Jeans. His shoes were blue and looked like Keds or Chuck Taylor's. Maybe they were Vans. Perhaps this time, he would have something to say. Maybe talk about the passion, his passion, anything, perhaps if she went first. "Hello. Do I know you?" As he had done before, he seemed to admire the craftsman details, and Mom thought he was not paying attention when he answered in thought, — "You have a very nice home."

Pilgrim Heights was built in the early century by a lumber baron. The basement was unfinished and had exposed beams from old-growth trees that were hundreds of years old when they were harvested when the home was finished in 1911. The attic has similar characteristics with no dividing walls. Stairs in the attic led to a Widow's Walk since the house once served as the official weather station for the area. The phrase Widow's Walk originated from the wives of mariners, who climbed on the roof to watch for ships to return and come into the harbor. This was often in vain in the early years, as the ocean took the lives of many mariners. Navigating the bar into Grays Harbor was treacherous enough, let alone sailing along the west coast and around Cape Horn before the Panama Canal was built in 1914.

"Who are you?" she wondered since he gave no indication or acknowledgment that she was heard. It's possible she had not said it aloud when he uncrossed his arms and grabbed the handrails of the rocking chair, pushing against them to sit up straight and planting his feet on the floor. He turned towards Mom, looked her in the eye, and opened himself up to conversation.

"You most likely do not remember me. It was long ago, and I wanted to thank you." — *Thank me?* Responding without words but using her eyes to communicate. He cleared his throat and began to rock in the chair, back and forth, keeping a perfect rhythm like a metronome.

Mom sensed something about him when they made eye contact, but she lost the thought when hearing the chair give its usual creak. This was where we were fed and rocked to sleep, often having a child needing a bottle, and at times the feedings were constant. She understood about keeping her babies rocking in the same soothing motion, often to the rhythm of the radio, until into the bed they would go, only to be awakened when another hungry baby would cry out, asking for their momma.

He leaned in so she would hear him better. He could tell when she was drifting, and she was drifting, thinking back to the early years and the rocking chair. What he wanted to say was important. He cleared his throat again and spoke emphatically.

"Do you remember telling me I would need to find a way to reconcile with my family at some point?"

Mom shook her head. She didn't remember.

"You were right. It took me a while to understand how to get there, and I had resented my mom and dad for splitting up. After meeting you and your family, I told one of your children I adopted you as my mom-like role model."

"Thank you," she said, appreciating the compliment and finding this interesting. But she still could not remember him, certainly not as a regular at the house, which made her curious.

She ran a hard drive scan, thinking of the countless people who had gone through her home—so many youngsters. Especially on the days she baked Rocky's Pizza washed down with Acidophilus Milk. The kids' friends, particularly Gibby, always seemed to know when it was pizza night and take and bake – an easy and popular solution for a dinner of eight or more. Even we boys could pop that in the oven, take it out and slice it up. In the late 70s and early 80s, our home was a revolving door of kids coming and going at any time, including all hours of the night. Could it be one of the 22 kids from the Gonzaga Prep Glee Club that stayed with us for a few nights in 1975 or one of the cast members from Up with People? We hosted performers back in the day. Or he could be any of her children's friends who came and went. She was a mom to Waldo, Fish, Reggie, Chape, Raj, Dr. Fu, and even the Mayr kid. They all ate, drank, and or slept over on weekends in those days.

Mom heard him clear his throat and turned her attention that way. Maybe it was an intentional scoff-type cough. Not scoff as in ridicule but combined with a smile as if reminding her he was still there. He was finding his voice, and Mom was drifting off again, so maybe it was both – he needed to clear his throat and politely get her attention back.

"The way your family helped me was when I needed it; this impacted my life and gave me a direction to follow."

This was when he was 19, had just got out of jail, and was reduced to couch surfing and banking on friends for a bed and even rumored to have been sleeping under bridges or in a box on Dale Crover's porch. The legends have grown over time. He was opening up, and Mom was enjoying the conversation, thinking how nice it was to have someone to talk with. Lately, she had been spending more time than not resting in bed. He went on to say that someone in our family had protected him and that we had stood up for him in an undisclosed way. "Protected me," was how he described it. She knew it would take one of her boys to answer this question.

Years later, this was the best explanation we could come up with when trying to answer how we had protected him. Any of us would team up to turn a bully away in a school hallway, classroom, playground, ball field, or if a weaker student was getting picked on. Old Timer and Balboa may have stood beside him and never remembered telling someone to get lost. They were the same age. I never recall anyone from our family being accused of bullying. Mom would have killed us because this was not in our nature. Here is another example from my older years.

Once at a party north of the Young Street Bridge, on the way to the cemetery, riverside specifically, I felt the need to stand in like a referee when I saw the making of fisticuffs in the front yard. Things looked one-sided; a scrappy underdog was squared up against one dude with two friends standing behind him, so I grabbed a club from under the front seat of my Super Beetle and stayed ready should things go sideways. This fight never came to big blows or headshots, so the disagreement was settled without incident. As a family, we could never fully explain that one compared to what he brought up next.

The visitor then described a building that was on fire. He said someone from our family was involved and some apartment building. The location could have been more specific, but he mentioned California. The only one of us that had previously lived in the state was the youngest brother, Spud. In fact, when he said goodbye to So Cal and returned home, his friend Dot began to refer to him as Hollywood in memory of his time there, so we called him both names for a while.

Hollywood was able to answer this question in a big way. There was a fire in an apartment building near where he lived with his roommate Harless. He recalled Yucca Manor as either the location of the fire or the apartment he lived in. When he saw flames across the street, he screamed and yelled outside the burning apartment, trying to warn people. However, Spud wanted to be clear "I never entered the building." Hollywood described his place as having fold-out beds from the wall, like in Laverne and Shirley. So did Harless when I ran into him at Guitar Galactica in Aberdeen.

Later a couple of girls came around the corner and asked my brother if he were the one yelling. They said they were almost trapped as the fire spread, and had they not heard the hollering, they would not have gotten out. It seemed the fire escape was blocked or something to that effect. Maybe it was the work of convicted serial arsonist and murderer John Leonard Orr, who was arrested about then.

Spud didn't think much of it at the time, just doing the right thing, and Hollywood never spoke of this with any of the family after he moved home. Nor did he remember a fire when talking with Mom at the lake the month before her death, as he remembered it much later. There is another theory on this one. The visitor could have been sending a warning as just after Mom died, my brother's apartment building caught on fire, and he lost most of his pictures and possessions. The nickname Hollywood didn't hold for long, and we were soon back to calling him Brother Spud, associated with the 1986 slam dunk champion Spud Webb at 5'6".

Mom closed her eyes for what seemed like just a few seconds, maybe a short nap, she was starting to lose track of time, but to her, it was, just like that, when she realized he was gone. Lying in bed, she thought she could smell a cigarette, and smoking is prohibited on the porch or inside the house. And then it happened, like times you have experienced yourself when the brain makes the connection. Mom had a flashback to another point when she'd smelled cigarette smoke in the house. The memory popped like the lid on a stubborn pickle jar when she remembered asking Spud and Old Timer if they had started smoking one summer. Pop went towards that jar again as she remembered when Dad found the blanket and pillow in the basement. Mom was getting it now; was she ever.

There was a boy who came to the porch around then. I remember talking to him. His eyes, yes, those pale blue eyes. This is the same boy. It really started to register, "I know it." The young man from my room is the same boy with blue eyes from the porch.

Chapter Six

Life in the '70s

Star Date: 1973 - 1980

Front Spud, Old Timer, Turk. Back Joey, Balboa

~*~

We were blessed with a terrific Mom growing up and as adults. Anyone who met her would say she was a kind and gentle soul who only lost her cool when it came to the frustrations of raising her children. Mary Jo never worked outside the home from 1962 until she went to university around 1979. In those 17 years, she was a dedicated mother and wife while trying to maintain an individual identity. In the early years, she did all the cooking, cleaning, laundry, and clothes shopping as well as groceries, church and school, doctor, dentist, and optical appointments. You name it. She did it. I don't know how she did, I really don't—day after day, week after week, month after month, year after year.

Mom was our everything until we gained independence in our teens, and the oldest brother Turk could take over some of the driving. She made sure we were up and ready to get to school. We were close enough that we walked every day, initially through the park, and later when we moved to the big house, we walked six blocks to the same school. With our move, we never changed schools or peer groups. We monopolized her entire life, and this was frustrating. Not that she did not love and support us; we got that 100 percent. But she was losing herself in this process.

It was at Pilgrim Heights that Mom started to give us chores to help her out. One task for me was to bring her coffee in the morning because I was pretty good at getting myself out of bed on the first alarm. The twins would sleep all day if she let them. Turk was also pretty independent with getting up and going, daily unloading the dishwasher – a job Dad says he did until he moved out. By the time I was 12, Mom had shown me how to turn on the washing machine, put in some soap and then move it along to the dryer when done. Not long after learning to do my laundry, Mom turned me on to ironing and mending. Because we grew quickly, pants often had to be let out, so she showed me how to hem my jeans, or I could turn them up and secure them with masking tape.

Mom was an excellent cook; we were a meat and potato family early on. We always sat down as a family for the dinner meal with assigned seats. We said grace, "Bless us, O Lord, and these Thy gifts, which we are about to receive from Thy bounty. Through Christ, Our Lord, Amen." Dinner was served family style, with the main dish and sides passed from right to left. When completed, you asked to be excused. Milk was a staple. Spaghetti was always pre-mixed with the sauce, so when we went out and poured the sauce on top of the pasta, we would not eat it. Not as good as Moms! Cousin Mike said the same thing about Aunty Pat's spaghetti. Maybe the sisters shared family recipes.

Regarding birthdays, Mom went out of her way to make sure it was special for us and would make us the cake of our choosing. In the 70s, it was the round triple-decker cakes, and by the 80s, she would be making a large sheet cake. We hosted a party with our friends at least once, but this was rare due to the six of us and the expense. Usually, it was cake and ice cream and a dinner of your choosing with family and maybe one or two local friends. There was always more than enough cake and ice cream for the regulars and leftovers for the next day.

One of my strongest memories is one I carry with slight regret. Mom spent lots of time preparing the dinners and would continue to wait on us even as the meal began being served and, in many cases, devoured. We would conclude long before she finished, often leaving her alone at the table after we excused ourselves. She would slowly and methodically enjoy a glass or two of wine. It is easy to look back at all the lost moments you wish to change, but that is a powerful memory, leaving Mom alone at the table with no one to talk to about grown-up stuff and the day's events. In retrospect, maybe the glasses of wine were a good thing.

Thanksgiving and Christmas were big days for us, often going out of town to visit the grandparents and our cousins in Tacoma. On three occasions, we drove to Missoula, Montana, to be with Aunty Pat and her family. Tacoma was a little over 90 minutes away, and Missoula was 563.9 miles away – 9 hours straight without stopping. We often stopped for gas and a restroom break, maybe a sandwich wrapped in wax paper pulled from the Coleman cooler. Back then, the car seat and seat belt laws were lax. Dad said one trip Joy Scout was held by Mom and nursed most of the way. I think that was the year we only made it one hour out of Missoula and had to stop because the pass was closed. Could you imagine traveling with six children and two adults in one vehicle?

At Christmas, the entire family would go to church together on Christmas Eve, and then we'd head home for presents. All the kids would be told to wait in the TV room and to keep the door closed. We learned this was to give our parents time to finish wrapping the presents before Santa's gifts magically appeared under the tree. We never spoiled this for the younger kids, but we older ones were on to Mom and Dad and that Santa dude. How old were you when you realized Santa was not real? Were you sad? Maybe at first, until you realized it did not matter because there were always more presents under the tree than just the one from Santa.

Joy Scout, Mom and Balboa holding guitar.

From my perspective, we were living the high life in our younger years. For Mom, it was a little more challenging. Dad would agree. "Can you imagine a person who was raised with no brothers and a father who was mostly absent from her life, being thrust into a world and environment of five boys?" adding, "It was as if she were the 24-hour-a-day director of the YMCA, combined with no breaks and the laundry and mess hall to operate." She had Joy Scout, too, but with six offspring, she must have faced the grim reality that her children had taken over. I get it now. Mom recognized she had little to no life of her own.

At times she must have felt defeated by her church and its position on birth control and the exclusion of women in leadership and ministry, yet this did not deter her. I remember her strongly advocating against getting married until after turning thirty. From an early age, there was a determination to gain personal independence and grow as a person, even while raising a large family. Mom was futuristically progressive compared to her church, yet she was still referred to as Mrs. Ronald Hulscher as if she did not have an identity.

In 1973, a married woman could not get a credit card in her name without permission from her husband. Imagine that. But times were a-changing when Congress passed a law prohibiting credit withholding based on sex, marital status, race, creed, color, national origin, or age. Soon after, Mom signed checks and notes of absence to school using her full name. Mary Jo Hulscher and credit cards were regrettable for Dad. However, not so, any debt accumulated early on was more than washed clean on the return on her investment in a little-known coffee startup—the one with the mermaid on the cup, the one that got its start in Seattle. You may be familiar with Starbucks. We will get to that later. We were still in 1973 when the Battle of the Sexes match was staged between Billie Jean King and Bobbie Riggs. Mom loved tennis, so you can bet she sat us in front of the television to watch this historic event. It was inspiring when Billie Jean won. Mom ensured all her boys knew our sister Joy Scout would have no limitations on what she could accomplish.

July 13, 1968

6

THE ABERDEEN DAILY WORLD

Mrs. Fred W. Berken, Women's Tennis Club chairman, left, jots down Mrs. Ronald Hulscher's score for the day after a morning of their favorite game at Samuel Benn Park. — (All tennis photos by Rich's)

The Daily World - Richard Edwin Short Photographer

Mom disagreed with the direction of teaching youth abstinence over a more common-sense approach to the curriculum. It was well before the years of sexual activity for me when she screamed in frustration that we were "never to have six kids" and that if we were ever going to have sex, we would need to "use a rubber." Balboa says she ran into her room (slamming her door) right after yelling this and took a little time out. I was a little lost on what she was talking about, but Mom always had a book or two around to help explain things to us, and I could always ask my older brother what a *rubber* was. Kids are never too young to learn the gross stuff that grown-ups do in the dark, and if you tell them not to or ban them from reading certain books, they will do it anyway. Or so I have been told. Mom never withheld learning the truth about life, biology, and science with books on every subject in the universe, including the original Google search engine of our time called the Encyclopedia Britannica.

Just as we were taught about the beginnings of life, we learned of the end of life when her dad Papa Joe died. Is it odd that I do not remember anything about the time? Was it because I was only eight years old? I have no memory or recollection of the funeral. Dad said that back then, kids did not go to funerals. But I remember another funeral from volunteering to participate as an altar boy, knowing I would get paid to ditch school. I remember that funeral. I have never been able to forget it—permanent image burn-in. There are moments in your life from your childhood you never forget. A first kiss, a schoolyard crush, the smell of the pavement after a quick shower on a warm day after the said kiss, or the first time you came face to face with the dead.

My job was easy. Leave class and walk a block away. All I had to do was hold the crucifix on a pole when we walked in from the back of the church and stand at the head of the casket when the priest whisked the incense around at the end. Easy Money. Soda Pop City. However, I had not anticipated the open casket and found myself looking down at the head of a corpse for the first time. I made eye contact with the mother and her two children within the congregation's full view. The mom held them together while they were all crying. I looked down again at the corpse and started crying, sniffling at first, then full-fledged bawling in front of everyone. Soda pop city became a tear-drop city. The priest gave me $3 before I headed back to class. They could not pay me enough. Dr. Fu can serve the next one. Learning my lesson, I hugged Mom, vowing never to repeat that mistake. Not the job for me. Instead, I shared a paper route with my twin brothers for extra cash.

We attended St. Mary Catholic school through grades 1st - 8th, and then we were turned loose in the public school system. We could not get away with anything because our parents were very active in school and church. We were always involved in sports programs, often going straight from school to practice—flag football in the fall, basketball in the winter, and baseball in the spring. Mom arranged a carpool with the other moms if an activity was not on campus or nearby. That is what mothers did back then. Thank you. You did it very well. We were regulars at church. Only sometimes as a group, but you were required to attend your holy days of obligation. In the late 60s, Mom started requesting folk music during the Sunday service and was met with resistance. Dad said she showed up with a guitar one weekend and sat in the front row to make her point. Have you seen the movie Sister Act? Mom was influential in moving the church forward with music. Soon after, a choir was made out of parishioners, but at first, only for the Saturday evening mass. Dad was in the choir, so I would go with him and sit near the front row, borrowing some alone time from my brothers. By the end of the 70s, there was music that sounded like Simon and Garfunkel. I think their names were Glenn and Doty.

Our house, as you might expect, was loud and full of the things that brothers do. We beat up on each other every day, chased someone around the house and yard, and found ways to bring on the hurt. The Old Timer ran through the yard and threw a butcher knife at his twin Balboa. Turk decked me with a left hook and accidentally body-slammed Spud when he was playing Portland Wrestling. Over time, Spud became frustrated because his brothers were all bigger than him. That did not stop him as once he chucked a croquet ball at my face from two feet away. By the grace of God, I miraculously caught it. Joy Scout thought it was cool to have brothers and would wrestle as she saw on the TV, deploying her favorite move. She sat on you and announced, "Gut Buster!" dropping all her weight via her buttocks and simultaneously knocking the wind out of you. Yes, we were a lively bunch; even the youngsters got in on the action.

Mom was too busy most nights to watch much TV, but in the 70s, some of us watched primetime shows such as The Brady Bunch, The Partridge Family, The Love Boat, Happy Days, and Laverne and Shirley. After Fonzi jumped the shark, we got the new channels, M-TV, when they played music videos, and HBO, where

I would sneak into the tv room to watch late-night movies such as "The Hollywood Knights." This was when our Mother displayed her superpowers. Maybe all moms do. They walk into the room only when something inappropriate is on the screen. It might be the only boob you saw all show, but that would be precisely when Mom walked into the room. If it weren't brief nudity, it would be the only part when there was a swear word, or what we called a "cuss" word. Back then, "shit" was a bad word. Now there is good shit, bad shit, and of all things, Holy Shit! Swearing was not welcome in our home. I always feared Mom marching me into the water closet and giving me a second swirly. One was enough.

Dad always gave straightforward advice on this subject, emphasizing "swearing should be reserved for special occasions, like when you hit your thumb with a hammer," or when I observed Mom stepping on a Lego. This has been excellent advice to follow through the years compared to how some folk frequently drop "f-bombs" today. I learned from Dad that swearing loses meaning if you use it regularly. He was right, like much of his advice, so save it for a good occasion. The other thing, attending the Catholic School, you did not want to end up in the principal's office. Ms. Dispenza would pick up the phone and give Mom a call. You did not want that to happen. We were fortunate as Ms. Dispenza ruled with a warm heart, suitable for a hug or a pat on the back. Let's say there was not a lot of swearing happening inside St. Mary School, but as for the playground, that was another story. I enriched my vocabulary by learning new expletives, some even in Spanish. I would bet playground swearing was another universal law in life.

~ * ~

Between 1970 – 1975 the Cobain siblings were as playful and entertaining as our family was, with stories of typical behavior between brother and sister. In a recent documentary, "Montage of Heck," Kim Cobain was interviewed and described the early years with her brother and life in the household on East 1st Street.

Kim described her brother Kurt as happy and playful until she reached an age where she could get into his stuff, play with his toys, and accidentally break things. As siblings, you remember how this made you feel because if a toy was going to be broken, you wanted to be the one that did it. Through the years, Kurt found ways to pay her back and "tormented" her by moving things around in her room as he knew she would be upset due to her OCD nature of having everything in its proper place. Similarly, I would take things from my brother's rooms and wrap them up as birthday presents. When Kurt discovered his sister was claustrophobic, he would cover her with a blanket or sleeping bag and hold her down, including but not limited to sitting on her head and "cutting the cheese." We would never do that. From there, Kim planned ways to get back at him "ten-fold," even taking the knob off the tv so he could not change the channel as an act of retaliation, forcing him to watch Captain Kangaroo. Sounds like my kind of sister.

One of her first memories of her brother is around three years old. A knock on the door immediately followed Kim and Kurt, running into the house, so their mom Wendy answered the door only to find a police officer standing there. It seems young Kurt had talked his cute little sister and her pink dress into flipping off the cops as they drove by their home. Kim described how Kurt was fascinated with flipping the bird and would flash the middle finger at other cars if someone looked at his Mother the wrong way. His protection and affection for the maternal were evident at a young age. I may have encouraged my brother Spud in similar ways, throwing bark chips at passing cars and then running into the cabin to hide when the car we hit was an off-duty state patrol officer, and he came to the door to tell Mom. Fortunately, all we received was a lecture.

Throughout this interview, Kim smiled when describing life with her older brother leading up to their parents' separation a few years later. They sounded similar to the rest of us at this point in their lives. It is evident the love shared between brother and sister and how they ultimately relied on each other to get through life in the years that were to follow in the East 1st Street Home.

Cobain childhood home.

Columbus Park on Black Lake

~*~

In 1971, Dad set Mom up with this killer, lime green Chevy Kingswood Station Wagon. She was the beauty that would serve us well for years to come. Mom being the beauty, the serving carried out by this luxury cruiser we passed down from each student driver until its death at the end of the 80s. Besides a Chevy Wagon, Pops found the perfect outlet to help everyone in the family, especially Mom, by scoring an extended lease on a cabin in Columbus Park on Black Lake – just an hour away from home. This would give us plenty to do instead of fighting each other around the house. We could fight each other around the lake, and Mom could stay home and find some peace.

The word cabin conjures a rustic and charming image, but this was a simple two-bedroom cabin with a rectangular ranch layout. One bedroom housed Mom and Dad, and the other had two queen-sized beds. Four could sleep in those two beds if you felt like sleeping beside one of your brothers. Otherwise, you could sleep in the attic, couch, or lawn chair with a sleeping bag. It had a fireplace for heat, running water, a bathroom, and a shower. We did not have a shower at home, only two bathtubs, so having a shower at the lake was cool beans. Joy Scout remembers the small cereal boxes you would tear open—where you pour the milk directly into the package. We ate boiled hotdogs and Kraft Mac n Cheese made from the box, with butter and milk. Peanut Butter and Jelly and a loaf of bread were always a staple.

The lake had an ample supply of fish called perch, which are very boney and best filleted. They were so small that, in reality, two fillets were just enough for a sandwich. We ate a lot of perch back then, pan-fried in crumb batter. Us kids were experts at catching them (56 one weekend). Dad was an expert at cleaning them, and Mom was an expert at cooking them. By the end of summer, we were tired of eating them.

A cool feature of the cabin was that the main entrance was a Dutch door in two parts, so you could open the top to create a nice breeze. Mom would stand at the door with the top open and drink her coffee. Just outside the door, we would line up our fishing poles, and there was a picnic table to sit at and a lawn chair or two. Above the Dutch door was the Sleepy Hollow sign. When Dad sold the cabin – the land lease was ending – the sign was fortunately taken down and stored in the big house. I found the sign in the attic 15 years ago, and it is now in my kitchen above the cupboards. Every time I see it reminds me of family fun times at the lake, and I get a little Mom juice thinking of her mom smile.

The cabin had an old ice box (refrigerator) and a washer and dryer. They were from the dark ages, but they worked. We mostly hung our laundry out to dry in the summer sun on the picnic table and wore the same clothes as long as possible. Dad says Mom never sent us to the cabin for a week alone, saying she would never have left the wagon there as she needed it, so I guess the reality was she would load us up and drop us off with the goodies for a few days. Dad may not remember, but once Turk turned 16 and could drive, we would go alone because Mom had the Honda. Either way, I remember a lot of unsupervised time at the lake – it was the late 70s and early 80s, with no internet, no cell phones, only a landline, and you were trusted to be on your own.

We spent entire summers there fishing, swimming, and watching whatever channel the black and white TV could pull in, all three of them. Perry Mason at noon was a staple. The radio played all the AM classics of the era. It was around when Turk purchased the debut BOSTON album when FM radio surpassed AM in listenership. Soon after, the cabin radio was dialed to 99.9 KISW, the Rock of Seattle. We explored, had popsicle stick races in the creek, and collected beer bottle caps to count out the most popular beer. Miss Budweiser (hydroplane) almost always won. The local Olympia and Rainier beers were popular. Lucky Lager beer caps had a puzzle on the underside, so those were popular finds.

~ * ~

We were on our way to the lake one time when us little donkeys made Mom so mad that she had Dad stop the car on the highway. She screamed, "Stop the Car," and that's what Dad did. She got out somewhere near Elma and started walking. Our Chevy Kingswood Station Wagon, lime green, stayed about the length of a football field behind her, idling along when someone stopped, and we saw our mom get in a stranger's car. The little donkeys got *vewy vewy* quiet. Elmer Fudd quiet. Dad was not happy. Imagine that. I don't think we had much to say the rest of the way to the cabin. Thank goodness Mom was not picked up by the serial killer Ted Bundy. He was known to have been around Olympia in the mid-70s and frequented the Evergreen State College, only 20 miles away. She made it to the cabin okay on her own, and we never forgot the day we saw our mom get into a stranger's car. This memory was certainly etched in our minds for eternity.

But that's the only time I remember her upset at the lake. Mom loved swimming, so we all took swimming lessons. The lake had a platform in the middle, about 10 feet in the air. She would sit on the shore and rate my dives with advice. I do not remember Mom getting in and swimming much, except taking her little Joy Scout and Spud in the shallows. Nowadays, you see a lot of kids wearing floats on their arms or life jackets, but back then, you had to learn to tread water or float on your back if you got tired on your way to shore. Mom and her lifeguard skills taught us how to survive in the water, just as much as our rescuer taught us to get through life out of the water.

The lake gave Mom some serenity. We were outside, free range, and didn't have to be driven anywhere, disappearing for hours. There was playing in the creek, fishing, and, as we got older, hanging out by the water so as to "scope out the Betties," with Betty being slang for a pretty girl who hangs around the beach. Going to the beach had the same impact on me as the lifeguard Wendy Peffercorn had on Squints Palledorous (and his black-framed glasses) in the movie "The Sandlot" with all the oiling and lotioning, lotioning, and oiling that was going on. Squints could not take it anymore and dove into the deep end, where Ms. Peffercorn saved him. He could not swim, creating a magic moment.

Fighting among ourselves was normal until someone tried to mess with one of us, which is another one of those universal laws in life. One time we were fishing on the dock, and a guy pushed Turk into the lake fully dressed. As my brothers pulled him from the water, I instinctively grabbed the guy, threw his ass down, and banged his head on the dock until he ran away crying. Later that kid's older brother came after Turk to even the score, although we felt the score was already even. We could mess with each other, but you better not come after any of us. The other family played by the same rules, so we understood well enough to leave things alone for the summer. Other than that, I do not recall much fighting at the lake. We knew to avoid the older kids having a good time drinking beer. There is an entire book we could write about our summers at Columbus Park when we became the older guys drinking beer, but the older we get, the less we talk about, or is it the less we can remember?

Copyright Pabst Brewing Company.

Spud recalls company picnics that took place at Columbus Park. The Olympia Brewing Company Picnic was the big one since it was headquartered in Tumwater, just a few miles away. We would sneak into these corporate events and get free hot dogs, ice cream, and soda pop. If someone asked us, who is your dad? We said Johnson, Smith, or Jones. If we used a name like Rutledge or Zelasko, they would not believe us as those names sound like attorneys, or they grow up to become one. Spud would win the running races and score pretty well in the haystack game, where hay would be spread over a tarp, and rolls of coins would be unwrapped and thrown in. His brothers coached Spud – we told him, "The coins will settle to the bottom of the tarp. Grab the quarters and half dollars first." He was the best in his age group, filling his pockets and running back to the cabin to store his loot, which he likely later spent in the park candy store on Jolly Ranchers, Pop Rocks, Gobstoppers, or a classic Hershey Bar, eating it before it would melt on the walk home. Add a melting candy bar to the universal law list.

We never went on a huge vacation, like Disneyland or Hawaii. Our summers were spent at the lake or visiting relatives in Tacoma or Montana, well-spent family time. When not at the lake, Mom and Dad ensured we were kept busy, finding activities and events to keep us occupied. Summer of 1978, Mom created a memory to last a lifetime when she loaded the wagon and drove us to Seattle to see Star Wars. It must have been newly released because we had to stand in line forever. It was a theatre with brick on the outside, with some turned outwards, making the wall easy to climb with its little steps. We watched the bigger kids climb to the top while Mom stopped us from going any higher than five feet up. It was also a really good movie, something we had never seen before. As it was for millions of others, we became fans to the point where I took my kids out of grade school to see the new releases of The Phantom Menace and Attack of The Clones. And later, in Christmas 2015, my kids took me to the premiere of The Force Awakens.

The 70s were winding down when the boys put a hole in the wall playing Nerf hoops. Dad heard the ruckus, rushed into the room, observed the damage, and angrily tore the backboard and hoop off the wall. It was without hesitation when Turk coined the phrase "Daddy Dawkins," giving him the highest honor in recognition of Darryl Dawkins, who broke two backboards in the 1979 NBA season. That was our Pops. The old man got upset, we laughed, and Turk gave him his first nickname. Daddy Dawkins even fixed the wall on his own, or maybe Grandad and Uncle Rick brought the trailer down from Tacoma for some camel time.

~ * ~

Along with raising her family of testosterone-fueled boys and one girl, Mom pursued education, taking classes in the fall of 1979 at Grays Harbor College. She studied nutrition to the detriment of us kids. Old Timer remembered, "Growing up, we had all the junk food we could ask for, and then everything changed." Sugar cereal and white bread disappeared, and into our lives came whole-wheat spaghetti. Gross. Mom was now into health and the philosophy of holistic medicine. We have her tutor Dr. Myles Robinson to thank for that. He and his wife Elinor moved two houses down from us and became family friends. Cheers to you, Mrs. Robinson. When Mom found no daycare for young children at the college, she took Joy Scout to class with her—Just like when she took a guitar to church to make her point— Typical Mom. She worked her magic with the college; the next thing you know, they set one up, and, in the end, she worked part-time as a daycare person.

GHC parking sticker on Pop's 57 Chevy

Chapter Seven

Pale Blue Eyes

Star Date: May 1997

Bridge Over Troubled Water by Simon and Garfunkel plays in the background as we drop into Mom's bedroom, where she finds herself deep in thought. This is a continuation of the experiences she has learned from her visitor.

Mom was controlling her breathing and meditative when thinking about his eyes. There was something about them. It gave her a warm feeling, not the least troubling, yet curious to learn more. As I remember her life, this is the way of the world, always seeking to understand. For Mom, curiosity was a path toward empathy, and with compassion came an understanding. Seeing his eyes when he pulled his hair behind his ears was like deja-vu. She had seen them before. Eyes are like the window to the soul, or was it a gateway? Mom understood the eyes showed more than what someone could see. They often were an indicator of how we think and feel. It always worked that way with her boys when she would look us kids in the eyes.

This thought made me chuckle in agreement, thinking about how mothers seem to have that extraordinary power to look kids in the eye and know immediately if they are telling the truth. This took me back to when someone was lying about eating Halloween candy without permission, and there was the determination to get to the bottom of it when Mom schooled us early on — never to try and put one over on her. We understood that – ever heard the phrase "rue the day."

At the McKinley house, she dragged chairs in from the dining table to form a semi-circle in the living room and sat us boys down. Standing in the middle, hands expressively set above her waist, she made eye contact with each of us. First, Turk, then me, followed by the twins. It felt like an eternity as Mom deliberated, now with her hand on her chin, head moving slightly, yet her eyes never lost contact. Was it all of us in cahoots and holding out as a team, she asked herself, or was it two of us and there was about to be a sellout, someone would give it up. Maybe it was a solo artist who went out on a lam returning to Turk, who was getting an early start on learning how to bluff and use his poker face.

Sometimes I think she enjoyed watching us and extended the agony with intent, knowing that when we made faces at each other, the guilty party was about to get made. Her laser beam locked onto you, and someone's game was up. This time it was the twins. They wriggled, looked at each other, and made faces, which was it. Busted. Mom had them. Mom had all of us. Sometimes you experience the collateral effects of others, feel their pain and recognize how to avoid it in the future. Don't mess with Mom.

The memories of the semi-circle faded when returning to the thought of his eyes, something about those eyes. Who was this boy? Alone in her room, she took shelter from her thoughts. There were many. Drifting away for a moment, eyes resting.

But yet, what was it? No time for sleep. She knew she was getting closer to the point when she met him. The recall it's happening again, and like a detective, she was working it out. But this time, it was not cigarette smoke that made her pickle jar pop. It was marijuana. The universal smell of skunk. She learned of this back in 1971 at the Satsop Rock Music Festival, and just like that, Mom made the association and teleported back in time to the smell of skunk from the blue and gold bedroom. When was this? Circa mid-80s, when the older boys were moving on? Yep, that was it.

Mom was getting the picture, but it was like banging the side of the television in the old days when it all came into focus. Just a few days after the smell of skunk, the blue-eyed boy showed up at her home and knocked on the door. Yes, the boy from the porch. That was it. He was the boy from the porch. Her pickle jar was popping like a bag of popcorn as she drifted off when a hypnagogic jerk shook her awake, but just for a moment when she drifted off again. If you have experienced the feeling, you get it.

The bridge over troubled waters transformed into calm waters, easing her mind with the onset of deep sleep and the recollections of his eyes.

~ * ~

While we had a stable family dynamic, Kurt and Kim Cobain were experiencing a slightly different world when their parents separated. For the next three years, Kurt shuttled back and forth between the homes until his mother granted full custody to his father (upon Kurt's request), and he moved to Montesano. This sudden change in his family dynamic dramatically affected his personality. Interviews with his mom Wendy over the years have confirmed this point as the nexus for the beginning of the Kurt Cobain legends, describing how he went from a silly nutball going 90 miles an hour to defiant and angry. Over the years, the legends and myths have grown, including his life in Aberdeen, many of which unfairly characterized our hometown that was not true. Growing up, families supported families, and there were rec leagues for adults and neighborhood playgrounds for the kids. Things changed on the Harbor and Aberdeen when the timber industry ran head-on into a spotted owl in the '80s.

One of the myths about Kurt is that he would not give his total effort in sports to bring displeasure to his father. So much of what has been published has been misrepresented that it can be challenging to separate fact from fiction regarding this legend. Still, I have found enough information about his days playing Little League Baseball to show that what you've read on this isn't necessarily the truth. In the end, Kurt Cobain was a better athlete than his legend gives him credit for. We could rewrite that legend.

Chapter Eight

The Sandlot Days

Star Date: 1975 - 1982

Kurt Cobain - Age 9

~ * ~

Not long ago, I came across the photo on the chapter page on Pinterest. The poster claimed it was Kurt at age 12. He looked very young to me, and the word Elks on his jersey did not jive with me because, for one, at age 12, he would have lived in Montesano, and secondly, in the 70s, we had two little league divisions in Aberdeen, with enough teams to support both. The Elks were in the Timber Division, which placed him on an Aberdeen team in, instincts told me, 1976, when Kurt would have been nine years old.

I was fortunate to share the picture with the Meat Man (my best friend), who told me that our golf buddy King was on the 1976 Elks Little League team. They met at the first practice, drawn to each other. Both were nine and the new kids. During a round of golf, King offered that one of the first things Kurt said to him was, "The only reason I'm here is that baseball is my babysitter." This was due to changes at home, and his heart wasn't in it. King explains, "At times Kurt showed little interest in the outcome of the games," adding that otherwise, he did the everyday things we did back then, "attending birthday parties and hanging out in the yard." King still has the team photo from 1976, confirming my suspicions from the beginning: Kurt was nine in the Pinterest photo. I asked King from a financial standpoint, "Why haven't you ever sold the photo? It could fetch some pretty good dollars." He looked at me with a big grin, "Because then it wouldn't be mine." It's good to be the King.

King sharing his personal copy

The Elks won the Timber Division Championship that year, and the team photo was published in the local paper. Our team, Reiner's Sporting Goods, finished second and was one of only two teams to beat the Elks that year. In my research, I found the box score battery in that game which read "Hulscher, Baum, Wiseman, and Foy." I learned a lot of things in writing this memoir, including that Kurt got his picture in the paper at age 9, and of all things, I may have pitched against the famous music kid.

It may not have been the same for Kurt at nine years old as for us. Baseball was a constant in our life, playing it for hours on end like in the movie The Sandlot – unless we found some other trouble to get into. When we moved to the Pilgrim Heights home, we converted our backyard into a ballpark we later called Budweiser Field, using a wiffle ball for the short field and a tennis ball for the long field.

One summer in 1978, Bill Murray came to town and played baseball for the Grays Harbor Loggers minor league affiliate. A special Saturday Night Live episode, Things We Did Last Summer, was filmed. My friend King and his brother, Burger, were bat boys for the Loggers, and many locals made the show. Filming took place during an actual game at Olympic Stadium. After hitting a home run, Bill Murray retired from baseball and returned to a life of comedy, leaving the harbor behind to film the movie Meatballs. The Loggers won the NW League Championship that year. King once had a Polaroid picture taken with Bill Murray but traded it to a friend in exchange for some baseballs. This may explain why he will not let go of the 1976 team photo with Kurt, telling me, "Of any trade ever made, I wish I could take it back."

In July of 1979, Pops took all five boys to the MLB All-Star game. We sat behind the home plate, all good, but in the second row from the top. It was exciting for us boys to enter the Kingdome but exhausting when we climbed to the third deck. We were still going. We kept climbing, and then straight uphill climbing, 27 rows. It felt like Mt Everest when we made the summit. But! We were in the second row behind the home plate! Pops saved the ticket stubs and says they are worth more now than what he paid at face value in 1979. eBay has a graded stub listed for $400. How much did Pops pay? $10 a ticket. $60 bucks for him and all the boys. Aisle 309 Row 27, seats 11-16. Thanks for the memories, Pops. What could he get for all six stubs? Knowing my Dad, he will put them individually into an envelope and make sure we each receive a cherished moment of the time we got to see all our favorite Major League Baseball players.

I was the first to try out for Little League in 1975, showing up with one of those plastic mitts and a Pete Rose amount of Charlie Hustle. Pops clarified again, "Your brother Turk was the first to try out, but he only lasted a week in Pee Wee." Whatever (I love my Dad) — I could run and catch and was picked up by the Reiner's team as a 10-year-old and destined to play right field my first year, once made a crucial catch and another time missing the ball entirely and taking it between the eyes, smashing my black framed glasses. The coach loaned me a glove for the remainder of the season, and I tossed the plastic mitt in the trash. Two years later, I made the 1977 Timber League All-Star Team and was credited with a home run.

But as I remember, the play was a double-turned-triple turned to go for home with an overthrow, keystone cops, but the paper reported it as an inside-the-park home run. The first family home run until my younger twin brothers came to town as 12-year-olds.

The twins were blessed with August Birthdays, a plus due to the August 31 age cut-off, putting them almost a year older than teammates with birthdays later in the fall. Combined with early puberty, they had an athletic advantage. Old Timer hit one out of the park in his first at-bat, celebrating with a fist pump crossing second base. (Imagine Kurt Gibson, Dodgers world series in 1988) His frustration for a 2nd homer grew game by game when he watched his twin brother Balboa jack his first dinger, and then his second dinger, and then, my oh my – goodbye baseball, he jacked his third ball out of the park that year. Old Timer's first at-bat would be his only homer. They both had good seasons and made the 1979 Timber League All-Star Team.

Pops enjoyed a proud moment, keeping a newspaper clipping dated May 16, 1980, when two of us accomplished the same feat. At age 10, Brother Spud made the paper for hitting a triple, and later that night, Brother Joey did the same thing at age 15. Pops had the 8mm camera out, timed it up to record Spud's triple, and caught some warm-ups from the big boy field at Pioneer Park as filmed through the outfield fence. Brother Joey was an alternate on the All-Star team that year but only an alternate because his team lost the playoff for the championship. It was politics at play, as his coach would explain. "If we win, then you are in" for the All-Star team (wheelchair George would be the coach), and if we lose, the other team's coach (Buszer and Blevins) made the call. Dad sat me down and shared, "It's important to show up, work hard, and most importantly, not let it beat you." Coach Busz became a mentor, and even as an alternate, I went to every practice with a team whose ego outpaced their abilities, and they disappointed in districts.

On May 18, 1980, Mount St Helens blew up two days after the family triples. This was the big one. Fifty-seven people perished in the biggest of blasts, and you could see the ash plume rising from Pioneer Park. This was over a hundred miles away easily and reported around the world. "Where were you when the mountain blew" became a standard greeting. A week later, the mountain burped again, and this time Grays Harbor was not spared, and we woke up to a layer of fine grit pumice everywhere. We played baseball with ash on the grass for the rest of the summer, which was fortunate. Many ball fields east of the mountain were shut down for the season due to poor air quality.

Balboa got his nickname because he had the most power at the plate and could be a hothead occasionally. He was never afraid to mix it up with his brothers. At age 14, he got kicked out of both games of a post-season All-Stars doubleheader. The second time was for heckling the home plate umpire from left field. One would think the Ump must have had Rabbit Ears. Or maybe he remembered Balboa and wanted to save himself the headache of hearing his chatter the next time he came to bat. Pops says he may have been kicked out of the first game from left field. Either way, it was quite a feat to get the boot twice. The legend of Brother Balboa got its start somewhere. I say it was born on that day.

Joy Scout preferred activity over dresses, and Mom remained her champion as she signed on for the Charlie Brown Pee Wee team. By the time Little League came around, she had geared up a chest protector, shin guards, face mask, and was the catcher for the Lions while asking for a waiver requiring an athletic-supported protective cup. Tomboy is not a fair description of Scout; she was an individual the way Mom wanted her to be. Want to play baseball like your brothers, then so be it. Joy Scout shared another example, "Mom was very proud when I played baseball and went on to become an altar girl, a role traditionally held by a boy," adding, "She always told me girls can be whatever they want to and still be girls." Mom was "Just Do It" way before Nike. Come to think of it, sister Maria's initials are MJ, and I have the same birthday as Air Jordon.

Spud - Aberdeen Timber League All-Stars Age 11

In 1981, it was not surprising that Spud made the Little League All-Star Team. In his case, it was time to show his older brothers what this little engine could do. He made the All-Star team as an 11-year-old and the following year at 12. His picture above was on the front page of the sports section of the *Centralia Chronicle* Stealing home. *(Photo credit CC-Pops)* - Spud was the best baseball player in the family, and his older brothers enjoyed watching him play. As an in-fielder, he had mad skills and could find the ball on the diamond. He took a shot to the face one time that gave him a black eye and required stitches—tough kid, that Spud. My friend Dunbar played with Spud and reported through the years, describing his softball skills as legendary.

Kurt Cobain continued to play Little League Baseball, where legend says his Father enlisted him in a baseball team. Donald was one of the coaches. It was even reported that his son would strike out intentionally to upset his Dad. Not so. The truth is that by age 12, Kurt was an excellent baseball player. The 1979 VFW team in Montesano went 11-4, and he had a batting average of .325 going 13 for 40 at the plate with 7 RBIs and scoring nine runs. If you add his eight walks and two sacrifices at bat, you achieve a respectable .437 on-base percentage, above the team average. He also stole four bases tying for second on the team. In the field, he was only credited with one error.

A teammate of his was able to add a bit of context. "Kurt wasn't the happiest kid on the team but was a good athlete. He had a good arm and could turn a throw to first base pretty well." That sounded like an infielder turning two, and if he only committed one error, he must have had excellent hand-eye coordination. I also was made aware Kurt was naturally right-handed.

Learning this, I felt it is safe to put any myth about his athletic ability to bed. Did he strike out on purpose? Perhaps it felt that way at age 9 for Kurt when swinging a bat most likely felt like swinging an ax. Typical of many kids at that age. They called it chopping wood back then. The difference in size between a 12-year-old flame thrower would make any one of us tremble in the batter's box when stepping up to the plate at that age.

What about age 12 after he had grown a foot? No way, based on the stat book and his role on a winning team. Kurt made 50 plate appearances and only struck out ten times. By my math, he never whiffed on purpose. (K/ab + sac + bb) = 3rd best strikeout to total plate appearances ratio on the team. At age 9, Kurt was a Little League Champion. At age 12, his team finished 2nd place with an 11-4 record.

One of the central questions when starting to tell this story was understanding how it was that no one made the connection that the Boy from the Porch turned out to be Kurt. It sounds implausible, but at the same time, none of us ever remembered playing baseball against him in Little League, either. It might be time to start a new legend. Maybe Kurt Cobain was a good athlete, but the guitar was his driving passion. Legend says more than maybe. The Rock n' Roll Hall of Fame inducted it as fact.

1979 VFW	A.B.	RUNS	HITS	R.B.I.	SAC.	B.B.	H.P.	ERRORS	S.O.	S.B.	AVG/DAYS	2B	3B	HR	BAT. AVG.
GAME															
TEAM TOTALS	378	137	137	89	7	70	6	39	138	27	.328	49	1	7	.344
WIN = 11 LOSS = 4															
ANDREWS DANNY	45	27	17	6	0	(11)	0	3	(5)	4		10	(1)	0	.378
AYRES DANIEL	12	1	0	0	0	7	0	2	9	0		0	0	0	.000
COBAIN KURT	40	9	13	7	2	8	0	(1)	10	4		1	0	0	**.325**
DANIELS RON	(48)	(30)	25	19	0	6	1	5	14	3		9	0	(3)	.521
DANIELS TED	45	9	12	4	1	7	0	2	16	3		2	0	0	.267
DEMOSS LARRY	31	6	8	3	1	6	0	7	12	3		1	0	0	.258
GROSS DAVID	17	2	1	2	0	2	(2)	2	12	1		0	0	0	.059
HANFORD MIKE	20	4	5	5	0	6	0	3	10	1		1	0	0	.250
HANBURG RON	27	6	5	2	0	3	0	0	16	0		0	0	0	.185
MARSH ROD	(48)	23	(28)	(26)	(3)	3	1	2	7	(7)		(13)	0	(3)	(.583)
MERTZ RANDY	43	16	21	13	0	7	1	8	12	0		11	0	1	.488
QUADT GARY	20	3	2	1	0	4	1	2	15	0		1	0	0	.100

Pops found a error on the original score-card.

~*~

"Well, it took me 17 years to get 3,000 hits in baseball, and I did it in one afternoon on the golf course." — Hank Aaron.

"Never let the fear of striking out get in your way ... Every strike brings me closer to the next home run" — Babe Ruth.

"Baseball is ninety percent mental. The other half is physical ... Little League Baseball is a good thing. It keeps parents off the streets." — Yogi Berra.

"Swung on and belted ... I don't believe it ... it will fly away... get out the Rye bread and mustard grandma, it's grand salami time ... my oh my " — Dave Niehaus.

Chapter Nine

Into the World

Star Date: 1981 - 1991

Balboa - United States Army 1985 - 1989

~*~

Turk was the first to graduate in 1981. My older brother was less of a baseball player and more into basketball as his sport of passion. He made varsity but found himself sitting on the bench most of the time until one game, and he got hot, like really hot. Ray Ryan of the Daily World newspaper described it, "He started reigning in howitzers from roughly South Elma." scoring 11 points in the 4th quarter alone. I was listening to the game on KBKW radio and going ape nuts, "That's my brother, that's my brother." He inspired me to follow in his footsteps.

Turk earned a degree from Grays Harbor College (GHC) and later found work as an essential worker, delivering beer for Budweiser. He may have been the most popular man on the coastal route, and those holiday deliveries wore him out. Coincidentally, on another trip to the coast with his buddies, a Grays Harbor Transit bus driver reported that a group of fellas had mooned his bus. We had been unable to determine if this was Turk's posse or another group of posers until he recently owned up to it, sharing it on Facebook 40 years after moon gate. Back then, all we knew was he laughed hysterically when it made the local briefs. Turk said the bus was tailgating, and DNA results proved his innocence. It must have been some other poser, as it was not his butt in the window.

I graduated in 1983, and inspired by my brother Turk, I gave up baseball, switched to hoops, and played on the varsity basketball team. I sat on the bench with my friends, the blue team bombers. The highlight of my athletic year was trying to dunk it in warmups and when the bombers took it to the starters in practice. We won the league title, defeating our cross-town rivals Hoquiam, and advanced to state, losing in the round of 16. After graduation, I went to work for Sears in the already sinking South Shore Mall. In 1988, I earned a degree from Grays Harbor College before moving to Bend, Oregon, and a career in retail. After that, moving where ever the job took me. The harbor will always feel like home, and I appreciate it annually when visiting Pops, my family, friends, and Highland Golf Course.

Balboa graduated in 1985 and avoided college when he enlisted in the army (thank you for your service) and was stationed in Germany. His earliest letters home ended with "serving proudly." Within a year, his letters ended with a countdown to his release date and touted the strength of his unit's flag football and softball teams versus any war effort. A Fräu·lein took an interest in Balboa until he made it known he had no intention of getting married, thus ending her dreams of going stateside. He toured Europe one summer with Old Timer, hitting up some places familiar to each. After returning home, Balboa graduated from GHC with the fifth degree in the family before earning a bachelor's in accounting from the University of Washington School of Business. Years later, he made Mom proud and went to work at the Starbucks headquarters in Seattle, and after that, he did his best to emulate Warren Buffet with his ability to pick a stock winner.

Pabst Brewing Company

Old Timer graduated in 1985 and was the best golfer in the family (back then, anyway), competing on several teams that went to state. Pops allowed Old Timer to use his golf clubs. These were 1953 MacGregor M75W Persimmon Woods and Irons, a good set, only sold in the pro shops; Pops deferred his earnings from working at a driving range in exchange for equipment so Grandad could claim him as a dependent. $600 annually was the cap for a minor back then, so these must have been tour quality, mind you. One of his teammates is now the head pro at the home course. Locally we refer to Ronnie Espedal as the big handsome.

Old Timer earned a degree from GHC alongside his mother. Go, Mom. He was the first kid in the family to graduate from a fully-fledged university (Central Washington) and later earned a Master's degree from Seattle U. He was on his way towards a career in international finance, aided by two years of study in France. This may be an early reason why Mom treated him like the chosen one. Just as likely, it was because she loved to explore France, and her son could speak the language. In addition, Old Timer never got busted like his older brothers: a wise one, that brother.

Kurt Cobain did not graduate in 1985 because he dropped out of school when he learned he did not have enough credits to fulfill the requirements. Instead, Kurt took on odd jobs such as a janitor in his former school or doing maintenance work at the Polynesian Inn out in Ocean Shores when not tending to his turtles, playing guitar, writing songs, or working as a free hand roady when driving the "melvan" for his friends Buzz Osborne and Dale Crover. His passion for creating music had taken a significant turn.

By 1985, Turk and I had moved out and found party flats to throw a bed in and call home. We two, once-combative brothers, now enjoyed hanging out and winning the city league hoops championship for Fred's Auto Body, with some help from the Blue Team Bombers. With us two hooligans out of the house, it should have slowed down for Mom, but instead, the Old Timer had spent a summer in France with the Choisy family on an exchange program, and it was our turn to host a student. Mom enjoyed welcoming a second daughter to the family when Hélène from Montpellier, France, came to live with us for the school year and took on one of the vacated bedrooms. This sparked Mom's life, leading her towards international travel and a love of France. Thanks to modern technology, we stay in touch and say hello to Hélène and her life in France.

Spud graduated in 1988 after successfully playing hardball through high school, earning second-team all-league as a 2nd baseman. He went off to Hollywood for a while and eventually went to work for the State of Washington as a purchasing agent and lived off and on at our cabin at Black Lake. He also became a landlord buying a few houses and later investing in a van. He lived in it for a while, enjoying the van life and escaping civilization. The year before, he remembered when Joy Scout asked for and received her first drum kit. It must have created some noise. She was schooling her opponents on the basketball court while not taking drum lessons. One of my favorite big brother moments with Joy Scout was the time we were goofing in the driveway before a game, and I showed her the spin move I learned from AHS hall of famer Gary Gallinger. She used it that night to score 24 of the team's 28 points.

Joy Scout graduated in 1991, went to Mt Hood Community College, earned a seat as a jazz drummer in the Genesis Band, and spent a year at Portland State. She roomed with my family for a summer in Salem, Oregon, and was a big help to the young children. They loved to watch their Aunt play her drums in the garage, prancing around in circles as little kids do. She packed up from there and went into the jazz program at the University of North Texas. It was here that Scout became an acquaintance of a classmate, a promising young artist named Norah Jones, and her then-boyfriend. Later that school year, Scout ran into the boyfriend and learned he had moved on from the relationship stating he did not think Norah would amount to much.

Joy Scout later continued her education and earned her Master's in music from the University of Washington. Nationally she has performed in some very distinguished venues, including on stages in New York City and at the Women in Jazz Festival at the Kennedy Center in Washington DC. We're all extremely proud of her. Check out her website. https://mariawulf.com/

Homecoming Fall 1990. Joy Scout with Mark Bruener - Former Pittsburgh Steeler, Washington Husky, AHS 91, and St. Mary School Alumnus.

~ * ~

Mom loved that Starbucks story. Old Timer remembered the time she raved about the best coffee she had ever tasted and expressed how much she "really, really, really liked the company," so much that she bought stock early on after the $17 initial public offering for sale on the Stock Exchange, later selling it when Dad may have suggested it would be wise to pay off her credit cards if she intended to go to France again. After her trip, she had the foresight to buy back in with 50 shares for $1,060. That is how much she liked the company and the coffee. Balboa remembered Mom deliberating about this and reminded me that back then, it would have required the assistance of a broker to make a securities purchase. their official stock rating report advised Mom against this purchase. As for the long-term stock price? It kept going higher and splitting and going higher and splitting. Pops never sold her stock, says he never will, and eventually granted 50 shares each to the children. Her original investment, with stock splits and dividends, is worth $84,000 and climbing. This is a valuable lesson, as it is easy to miss the actual value of a growth story and fail to buy back in because you sold early. No one likes buying high and selling low, but this story was different, and Mom was on it early. The Old Timer said it best when he told me, "It is good Mom did not listen to Dad on that one." Balboa said the same about the broker.

TM Starbucks 2023

Chapter Ten

Ain't Got No How
Whatchamacallit

Star Date: 1984 -1986

~*~

At about this time, mid-eighties, the local police department went through a fundamental change in how they would address minors and alcohol on the Harbor. This was just after Mothers Against Drunk Driving took a platform, Nancy was in the White House, and the United States ended up with the disastrous policy of the War on Drugs. Let's say the shift was seismic in comparison to the years before.

In 1984, Congress enacted the National Minimum Drinking Age Act. Up to this point, if you were found with alcohol as a minor, the penalty was to dump it. If you were found in or near your car, you locked your keys inside and walked home. Soon after, they started to cite you with a $75 fine called a minor in possession (MIP, or minor in possession by consumption.) And, even if you didn't have alcohol on you, but the smell could determine it, the local police gave a citation. Soon they were giving them out like Halloween candy. It depended on the officer, as Turk later found out.

Aberdeen was a small enough town that most people knew everyone. Brother Turk and I were required to appear in court for one of these MIP citations, so Dad came to watch. Judge Parker was behind the bench. We went to school with his kids. The honorable judge made an announcement directed to "all the people in the audience," saying he thought "it is a travesty" that young men such as these were old enough to die in service for our country but were not old enough to have a beer, and pounded the gavel for effect, lowering the fine to $25. All the people in the audience that day consisted of Dad.

One of these MIP citations we called The Magnificent Eight. As you'll have guessed, eight at the Gentz flat on the south side were listening to music and sitting around bullshitting. We cranked one song loud. The record was Tom Petty and the Heartbreakers' Damn The Torpedoes on vinyl. The song was Refugee – side one, song one – incidentally, after Nirvana, Dave Grohl was asked to join Petty as a drummer but declined.

We turned the song down, but it was too late. The neighbors had reported us. (Enter Joe Friday, Dragnet Voice.) There was a knock on the door, an officer of the law. He checked our papers, shit, we were underage. There was a keg on the counter, an old one, and he drained it. (Exit Joe Friday.) We were very polite and cooperative, as each citation was individually prepared. I think one of us, Raj, most likely tempted fate and joked, "Would you like us to line up alphabetically officer?" immediately followed by Weedly. "Or would it be more helpful if we lined up by height?" Fortunately, Joe Friday was distracted by our antics and never noticed we had been drinking 7oz Miller Killers and other bottled beverages. Thrown off by the keg on the counter, he never checked the fridge, which was full of beer: just the facts, ma'am, just the facts. We grabbed fresh beers from the refrigerator with the officer gone and the coast clear. With the volume lower, the needle on the turntable dropped onto the 3rd song on side one. When the chorus hit, we cranked it up again —Even The Losers (get lucky some time). The magnificent eight signed a beer bottle in memory of the occasion. Malitzia still has it—our very first MIP.

At the same time, Kurt Cobain had a few run-ins with local law enforcement. Recently one of his arrests was reported in an interview with his very close friend Buzz Osborne, describing one of the nights Kurt ended up in jail. They were spray painting on a Tuesday and ended up near the corner of a bank when Buzz explained what I call the "scatter drill." That is what happens when you hear the sound of a cop car coming to a screeching halt, "errrrrck." They all *scattered* in different directions, but Kurt was nabbed and the only one arrested. He spent a night in jail and told Buzz the experience was "horrible." Legend says he was arrested for spray painting "God is Gay," but police reports note the phrase was "Ain't got no how whatchamacallit," a random word – whatchamacallit was a candy bar. According to the Aberdeen Police, Kurt gave a written statement.

"To night, (sic) while standing behind the Sea 1st Bank in the alley by the Library talking to three other people, I wrote on the Sea first bldg. I don't know why I did it but I did. What I put on the wall was *Ain't got no how whatchamacallit.* Now I see how silly it was for me to have done and I'm sorry that I did. When the police car came into the alley, I saw him I droped (sic) the red marker that I had used." (John Hughes & Ryan Teague Beckwith. *On the Harbor* pg. 181)

A year later, Kurt was cited for a MIP and trespassing when he was found climbing around the roof of an abandoned building just after midnight. He spent a week in Aberdeen City Jail. His fingerprint card shows the date of his arrest was May 18, 1986, but due to a failure to pay from his previous arrest for alcohol in Seattle and his poor financial situation, he could not make bail. He was released on the formal booking photo date of May 25, 1986. Previously Kurt had been staying with the Shillinger family while sleeping on a yellow couch. They brought him a pack of smokes while he was in jail to help with his nicotine withdrawals and later donated the yellow couch to the Aberdeen Museum. As the story goes, Yellow Couch has a second cousin. You will be introduced to Ghetto Toilet.

Please take note the paparazzi did not take the time to find my mugshot and fingerprint card and put those for sale on eBay following the time in 1984 the police put me in the Po-Po for attending an underage party. Pops and Turk came to bail me out. It should have been straightforward, except an officer in the lobby recognized Turk from the party and immediately took him to the ground. My brother says he was body-slammed. Pops says it was a headlock to the floor, Portland Wrestling style. The officer then issued a MIP citation. Why? Earlier that evening, this officer was at the back door of our underage party. Turk saw him and slammed the door in his face, taking off for another exit. Before he could escape, a different officer stopped him and checked his id. Turk was one week away from his 21st birthday. Because of this, the second officer let him walk out the door without a citation and wished him a happy birthday. Pops later sought legal advice from our neighbor

Frank to correct the wrong by serving Turk's citation in the police lobby. Charges in his case were understandably dropped as a MIP for slamming a door did not hold up in court.

Kurt endured similar petty charges that many of us were subjected to while catching a buzz or trying to find something to do with our time. The big difference was he did not have a dad who could call on a neighbor to help make things disappear. This certainly made a difference in my life compared to what Kurt experienced. I've included his fingerprint card from the May 86 arrest and never noticed this before. It looks like guitar string indentations on his fingertips created a deep recess, trapping ink during the booking process. I've also realized that the officer on the fingerprint card is the same officer who arrested Turk in the police lobby. Now that is Spooky. Better call the X-Files.

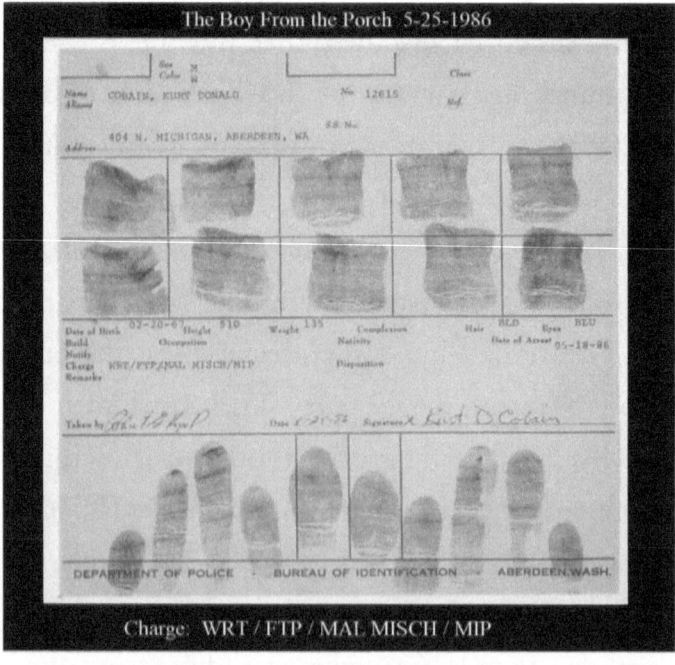

~*~

It was a year and a half after his time in jail when Kurt paid $152 in studio fees out of money he had made as a janitor to record Nine (9) and one-half song demos, which gave his music the exposure needed to sign a record deal. Why the ½ song? The tape ran out, and so did his money. He recorded his first album a year later, although it was frustrating when it was not released until June of 1989 by Sub Pop. Kurt found modest success with 40,000 sales from the first album Bleach, helped along by the interest in the song Love Buzz. It was the one song released as a single and reviewed by Melody Maker in the UK by Everett True. The world was learning his name when he released his second album Nevermind on a new record label (Geffen Records) two years later. By January 1992, the album had hit #1 on the Billboard chart. In April of '92, Kurt's picture was on the cover of Rolling Stone. He then appeared on Saturday Night Live, and hysterically the band members decided to "piss off the rednecks and homophobes" by making out with each other during the closing credits.

The following year Nirvana was the first to appear on SNL for a repeat performance, and as of the time of writing, Dave Grohl has the honor of being the most frequent musical guest on the show. Since his first appearance in 1992, Grohl has been a musical guest on Saturday Night Live 14 times—more than any other musician. He has appeared with Nirvana, Foo Fighters, Them Crooked Vultures, Mick Jagger and Tom Petty.

The Boy From the Porch we met a few years ago now had a legion of followers who worshipped his name. Kurt Cobain's world was turned upside down overnight.

At the same time, Mom was finding and enjoying her freedom while growing by leaps and bounds. She was coming into her own and became my best friend and even more to the family, if not the world. She had evolved from being our YMCA director and disciplinarian to our mother and spiritual guide, developing the vision and insight needed to sit you down and give straightforward advice without slamming the door. This was her time to shine, and she did. I was not the chosen one. That was the Old Timer, but I often asked her for advice. Sometimes she could be like Yoda, and you gained wisdom while she did nothing but hum to herself and give you the mom smile. That smile radiated love and warmth. Other times, like the Oracle, speaking to Neo in The Matrix, she just asked if you would like a cookie, and you felt better before you were even done eating it. I loved this about Mom.

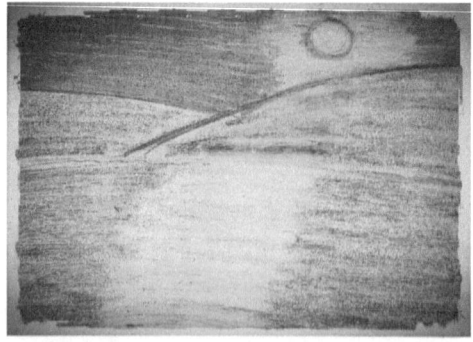

"Mirror Pond" ~ Author

Chapter Eleven

A Happy Schoolgirl

Star Date: May 1997

Moms Favorite Mountain

~*~

The Boxer by Simon and Garfunkel is playing in the background. We are back in the Bedroom of our mom. She nears the end of her life with little over a month to live. This is the third visit of four and is a dramatized visualization based on the events she described in the weeks before her death. On this visit, she is taken to places that had been very important to him in his life, as if they were clues and markers in time.

Mom was awake when the lovely young man returned. Afterward, it may have felt like a dream as her body wore down from her advanced lung cancer stage. Having never been a smoker, life was giving her an unfair go of it, a bad beat, as older brother Turk likes to say. If she had been a smoker, it was rare, if ever, and out of sight. As a child, Scout drew a picture of someone smoking. Mom pointed to the cigarette and asked, "What's that? — That's you smoking, Momma," The picture was ripped up as Scout recalled, and smoking was not something anyone could remember seeing her do again.

Mom did not remember him walking in the room but instead suddenly realized he was there. She asked directly this time.

"Who are you? — I think I remember you."

Once again, he did not answer her question directly but reached out his hand and said, "Would you like to see some of the places that were important in my life?" She nodded yes, like a happy schoolgirl, for on this day, she was feeling young – a rare occurrence of late. She grabbed a sweater and was good to go. But they did not go out the door. As she was bundling herself up, she felt a rush, and they went straight up as if they were in a giant helium balloon, and she found herself looking down at her house.

He pointed at the house on the hill and said this was where she helped him, and he thanked her again. From there, he showed her a view of the entirety of Grays Harbor to the Pacific Ocean, pointing out the nostalgic spot – Mayr Brothers Logging – and telling Mom, "I played there when my dad worked there." She thought he had played with her twin boys and the Mayr kid. His dad Werner took them there back in the day, and they would run around the log yard while he checked in on the weekend business. That was before the spotted owl happened in the 80s, and the industry was decimated.

They headed east. It was over the Muddy Banks of the Wishkah and then Think of Me Hill when he pointed down in that direction where he lived as they then headed out towards the Wynooche. She could see the cooling towers of the mothballed power plants and remembered attending the Satsop River Fair and Tin Cup Races in September of 1971. This was Washington's first legal outdoor Rock Festival that turned into a muddy mess. She blushed when saying, "My husband took pictures of the hippies in the river over there, and you know, some were even naked." This made him smile and nod in appreciation of her coolness. Were you there? But asking with his eyes. You can bet your *Wishbone Ash* she was, with pictures to prove it. She giggled, and they continued east.

They were both fond of Evergreen State College, so that was an easy next stop. Mom would take us there to swim and to use the high dive, and he said he would go there for music reasons. She was happy to tell him about the classes she had taken at university. He shared enthusiastically about doing his band's first demo recording one night, somewhere around midnight, on KAOS, college radio stuff, or something. He took Mom by a house in Olympia and talked about a girl he lived with.

They made their way to Tacoma and visited the little angels' section, finding the grave of John Joseph, then showing her where his band played at the Tacoma Community World Theatre. He made a spin over UPS, The University of Puget Sound, and her home in the Proctor District, by the Piggly Wiggly and the 7-11 to where we would ride our bikes with our cousins when we visited and felt the urge for an ice-cold Slurpee. They went to Stadium High School, where scenes from the movie "10 Things I Hate About You" would be filmed a decade later with a nod to Heath Ledger, who passed at age 28, eleven years after this flight.

Over Puget Sound leading into Seattle, as they turned right and did a few donuts around the Space Needle, he began going into detail about the history of music in the late 60s and Jimmy Hendrix. He said that just a few years ago, in the early 90s, the Seattle Music scene changed the world, and that was something that he was a part of. He showed her the Paramount Theatre, where he played. She could tell he was proud of what he had created, and then he showed her a couple of houses. One his friend purchased had a haunted basement, and the other was by a lake he had lived in most recently. It was then she saw Mount Tahoma in the distance. They took off like a jet over her favorite mountain and headed for Europe.

She described the next stop as the country that "looked like a boot." They flew through and visited the Roman Colosseum and three times around the Umberto I Polyclinic Hospital before he mumbled something about the Rome American Hospital and then jet-setted off over the Mediterranean Sea quickly as if he did not want to be there anymore. She saw the town of Montpellier and thought of her Hélène, the French exchange student who Mom considered a daughter, and then North towards Reims, where the Choisy family lived and hosted Old Timer his first summer living abroad. Mom was alive with her memories of France when these towns came into view, recalling her love of visiting the country.

Mom was getting tired when he took her back to America, Los Angeles, and his world there. He was rejuvenated, though, showing signs of life as he talked about the birth of his daughter Frances. The weather changed as they headed north toward Seattle, and Mom could sense cold and darkness. And then it started to get cold, the kind of cold that works thru each layer of clothing until there is nothing left but the chill of your bones.

They closed in on her home, and he dropped her off in her room, where he held her hand as she slipped back into bed and the comfort of her sheets. They smelled fresh, as if someone had changed the linen while she was gone. She looked up in time to see him leave. Like a ghost, he drifted backward and out the middle bedroom window, and just like that, he was gone, unsure of herself as it appeared he was moonwalking out the window as if making a nod to Michael Jackson, whom he knocked off the charts in 1992.

She took the time to recall everything and every location they had traveled to that day. It must be that music kid based on where they went and the things they had seen, places discussed, and memories shared. The one whose band impacted all those people. The one that was from our hometown. It must have been a spine-tingling holy shit moment when Mom put it all together and made the leap. Pale Blue Eyes is The Boy from the Porch – those two were the same person. Not only that, but they were that Famous Music Kid.

~ * ~

Mom described the visitor taking her to places important to him and his life. One would expect they spoke, but what actual discussion they may have had is still being determined. We were not there, but her comments mentioned going up like in a helium balloon over our hometown, Olympia, Seattle, the country that looks like a boot, and LA. The rest is based on accounts of what Old Timer overheard in the kitchen and from Spud. The tour stops on the way are based on first-hand accounts and are accurate to the life of Kurt Cobain and what mom remembered and shared with Old Timer and Spud.

Chapter Twelve

Angels and Demons

Star Date: 1992-1997

Mom and Kurt were following the same path in life at this time. His band was doing quite well, and both survived the challenges of the previous decade while entering what should have been their greatest of years. They were living parallel lives, with individual success and achievement occurring nearly simultaneously. Yet despite this success, they were both challenged by demons.

Something inside did not allow either to sit back and enjoy the rewards of their hard work. Mom had an unresolved conflict with her church over the lack of evolution in their teachings, both from a symbolic and realistic standpoint. She had other demons only shared with Dad. And he is not talking. As for Kurt, his sudden rise to fame and everyone worshiping his name created unrealistic expectations and pressure. These alone were enough to increase his affection for his addictions and the escape he found with his evil devil twin Boddah – his childhood imaginary friend to whom he penned his suicide note.

Kurt was a creative and artistic introvert, cast into the role of the voice of a generation, and there was no place to hide. People are writing letters from around the world. The Canadian band Sloan found abandoned fan letters addressed to him at Sub Pop in Seattle, which inspired the song *Penpals*. It would be best if you gave it a listen. You may have never heard of the band Sloan because Geffen Records refused to promote their second album, Twice Removed, in the States because it did not sound *Grunge* enough. Pressure to be the next Nirvana was felt everywhere in the industry due to Kurt's influence. Note: Twice Removed has been voted the best Canadian album of all time in 1996 and 2005.

Early on, Mom found her voice and was a frontrunner in opposing nuclear power on the Harbor, even taking her young Spud and Joy Scout to protest at the local Public Utility District power company, waving a sign that read, "No Nukes is Good Nukes." It was significant when in 1987, she graduated from Grays Harbor College, walking the ceremony with the Old Timer in another — way to go, Mom, moment.

She continued studying at Washington State University, St Martin's College, and Evergreen State College. This was an extraordinary time in her life. She became a sponge, tirelessly driven to soak up new information allowing herself to think outside the box of her long-held traditional church teachings. I get this from Mom. When she became interested in something, it absorbed and consumed her, taking up most of her attention and energy while engaging herself in the process of learning. Or, as in my case, writing this memoir.

Old Timer and Mom 1987 - GHC

Mom jokingly referred to herself as a heretic, so it was no surprise that Tarot signs and their meanings became an interest to her, as was the geometric influence in the European cathedrals. She became hooked when reading "The Woman with the Alabaster Jar, Mary Magdalen and the Holy Grail." This book, written by Margaret Starbird, among others, piqued her interest in the early history of Catholicism. From there, she began questioning the hidden elements and history of our beliefs and church teachings. She had developed a newfound quest for knowledge of the church's history, solid Catholic topics previously suppressed and rarely spoken of. Mom became good friends with the Alabaster author, so much so that Margaret came to our mother's funeral, she sought me out, "So, you're the Joseph," I don't know whether Mom spoke to her about me or if she was trying to ease my pain during the most difficult of days.

Mom loved books but read very few fictional novels in her adult life. Every book she read expanded her mind, including Shirley MacLaine's theories, connecting with her higher self, which led her to attend one of Shirley's workshops in Seattle. Around this time, she began to have deeper discussions with Old Timer and the evolution of her beliefs. It was enjoyable to have these discussions with her during this time of her life and surprising to him, considering the dogma of our solid Catholic upbringing.

One of the amusing things about Mom was that she lacked or disregarded political tact. If something bothered her, she asked a question that would bore to the heart of the matter, and the respondent could not escape the point until they answered the question. If you were ever on the receiving end of this focus and determination, you were sure to know it. A great example is the local hospital's lack of a pastoral care program. This was bothersome, so uncomfortable questions were asked, and a commitment was secured from those in charge. Mary Jo was central in creating the Pastoral Care Program at Grays Harbor Community Hospital. She would work as a chaplain while fulfilling the same role at the Aberdeen St Peter Kidney Dialysis unit. Go, Mom.

At the same time, she enrolled in Seattle University's Spiritual and Leadership Training program while working towards certification as a pastoral care chaplain through study at Virginia Mason in Seattle and St Francis in Federal Way. Old Timer remembers reading feedback from one teacher, telling me it was inflammatory and filled with pejoratives. It was as if they felt Mom would be unable to separate her personal feelings from her work in the clergy. That's so far from the truth of how our mom was as she continued to reach roadblocks with the role of women in ministry. Old Timer did not hold back, sharing that, in his opinion, it was as if the church felt that a woman of the clergy would be viewed as sacrilegious while hanging on to that last word as I scribbled in my notebook. Like Pops, he knew how to pause and hang on to a sentence until he found the right word to make his point.

I had long since recognized her natural gift of the ability to read people and, at the same time, tactfully give them the answers that they needed to hear. Sharing this gift with church members would have been extremely meaningful, but it was as if being robbed of this blessing and genuine and extraordinary talents were going to waste. Dad told me there was a requirement in the chaplain program to show efforts in making an impact with a cause. Mom picked a good one, trained as a domestic violence educator, and served on the advisory team.

Pops opened up on this subject, "This was something special about your mom that is important for you to know. By creating the domestic violence awareness and education programs, which would train the priests and ministers, Mary Jo was actively involved in confronting the church and its handling of domestic violence." I was picking up what Dad was putting down. Mom focused her laser beam on the expectation the church was putting on the wife in a Catholic marriage while hardly ever holding the abusive male accountable. Another *"Go, Mom"* moment for me. *You get them!*

When the film "Spotlight" was released in 2015, I thought of Mom and wondered how she would feel about a dark chapter of her church being made public and receiving global attention. She looked up to priests as father figures and held many in high regard. But she was not intimidated. When we were very young, she steered us boys away from a man of the clergy. Old Timer remembers her referring to him as "the mean priest."

In 2002, the Boston Globe Spotlight team began investigating priests who had been accused of abuse in the Boston area. The investigators used church directories as a compass. The reporters had developed a database showing that scores of active priests were being inexplicably removed from parish assignments around the time victims received secret settlements. The scope of the abuse was far greater than previously known. Fourteen years later, in 2016, under public pressure and increasing exposure due to the film, the Archdiocese of Seattle finally released the names of priests who had been involved or accused.

I asked Aunty Pat about this. She said she was aware the list had been published. I expected her to say, "Oh, nephew, why must you go there? Do you need a hug?" But we were on the phone, and instead, she said, "Your mother never brought anything up directly to me." Her following statement caught me off guard. "There were 77 names on that list, Joseph, and I could recognize 55 of them. Fifty-five names I remember having been around church and school the 12 years we attended St Patrick's and the Aquinas Academy, including some from the Bellarmine preparatory school for boys where your dad attended."

I was conflicted with the need to press forward on this issue as I did not doubt that our Mom would have found herself in difficult situations with clergy at different points in her life. Yes, I wanted to because when Granny Reed passed away in 1984, Aunty Pat remembers vividly how Granny kept saying, "I am sorry, I am sorry, I am sorry," to her sister Mary Jo. Still, she did not know what that was all about, offering in the end, "Joseph, you just never know these days now, do you, Nephew." — Now I needed that hug.

Our Mom never backed down from challenging the church in her lifetime, and she would want accountability regarding this ugly history of abuse. We must have difficult conversations to move forward on the path we were intended to take in the first place. Each of our scars is unique, and showing respect for these scars in the world's weight reflects our inner strength. Concerning our Mother's distinctive scars and inner strength, whatever Granny was sorry about, Mom took to her grave. As for other her other demons, Dad is still not talking.

Christmas on the Porch 1995

The end of a long day.

Chapter Thirteen

His Final Visit

Star Date: May 1997

A Hazy Shade of Winter – The Bangles' version- plays in the background. We are in Mom's bedroom; the end of her life is near. This is the fourth and final appearance and is a dramatized visualization based on the events shared in the weeks before her death. On this day, her visitor reveals details about his death.

Mom was in that hazy place between sleeping and what comes before wakefulness when the visitor returned for the final time. She found that his presence put her in a calm and peaceful place, feeling good when he came around, but this time recognized his appearance had changed. Gone were his cardigan sweater and the lightness of his being. There was darkness around his eyes as if he were withdrawn and sulking. He was wearing a sweatshirt with a hood, undoubtedly different and unusual. She tried to make out the name, but the letters were enlarged and inverted, like in a mirror. Snivlem maybe? She could see the word Prick in red letters. This was fitting, considering she had met a few of those in her years.

Maybe that was another reverse deja-vu message for someone to understand later that had been known to happen with Mom when she asked,

"Are you okay? You do not look well."

He shook his head in four different directions like Pops does when he does not want to respond to the question until he has all the answers arranged in his brain. The way the boy held his head, though, leaning forward with his forehead in his palms and avoiding eye contact, indicated that something was different. He was troubled and not the same as remembered from his earlier visits.

His voice trembled when he said, "I would like to talk about something that is not easy." She reached out to hold his hand but instantly became lightheaded, her mind foggy. He started to tell her something, but he was talking so fast she could not make out all the words, which were mixed and messy. It must have felt like going through a wormhole because it was as if she were getting audio and video clues separately but at the same time, only seeing what he was allowing her to hear and hearing what he was allowing her to know when the visualization and audio synced back up together at the same time she let go of his hand.

She could make out the house he had shown her in the Seattle area, the one by the lake. There were images of a badge, someone was holding a badge as if they were in a position of authority, but they were not a cop. This person was searching and or investigating something. He was an investigator. At that moment, her clarity returned. There was silence, a still silence when he stopped talking. A total awkwardness came over him. She had seen this before in people who had been in traumatic situations. This had something to do with the investigator.

He then said, "I need you to know something. There were drugs, confusion, uncertainty." He could not find the words when he paused. Mom could see it in his eyes when she encouraged him to be strong. "I took my own life, I ended my life, and I need you to know the truth about this investigation because it is causing harm to my wife and family." They were blaming his family?

He repeated: "This investigation is blaming my family."

Immediately, she could sense and feel this was not right. This investigation was a farce. He chose to end his life, and it was because of the drugs. The investigator is a farce, and he is hurting his family.

Yes, he said, "This is a farce." He repeated the word many times, like a record skipping in the same spot, "farce, farce, farce." It was as if he could not make his point enough, and then it died out like a beacon with a dead battery. The investigation of his death was a farce. He whispered something that only Mom could hear. They shared a brief moment as if he were saying goodbye when she found herself alone again in her room. He was gone. This would be his final visit. She took a few days to process her thoughts.

It was in this moment of reflection that pushed Mom to inquire as to why no one in the family ever mentioned his name. She attended school with the mother of a Seattle Seahawks wide receiver at Aquinas Academy, and Spud always talked about Paul Skansi because of that relationship. She thought that if he were this famous music kid, then Spud would have shouted "his name" like he did "Skansi" when scoring the game-winning TD against the Chiefs in 1990, and like when the local boy "Bruener" scored a TD as a freshman in the Rose Bowl. Mom was in Pasadena at the game, and Pops was going bonkers because we knew the Bruener family from church and school. Old Timer coached Mark in 6th-grade hoops. Nice people. This made no sense to her. No one celebrated his success or spoke of him in death. She wanted answers. Someone had to know something, and she would find out who.

Soon after, Mom found courage, said a bad word, *effing cancer*, turned the key in the Honda Accord, and made her way out of town. You heard that right, Pops, I love my Dad, but I must say it anyway to my Outer Banks friends and all those who agree — **fuck cancer.** Either way, Mom hit the road and was off to get those answers. First on her list? Old Timer and Spud.

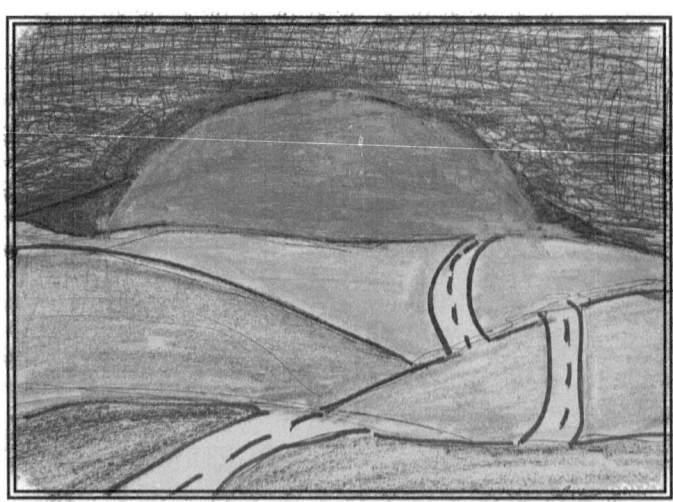

"The Road Home" GHC 1987 - Author

Mom with her grand-nieces, Haley and Colleen

Chapter Fourteen

Jesus Wants Me for a Sunbeam

Star Date: June 4, 1997

~*~

A song is playing in the background. Jesus Doesn't Want Me for a Sunbeam, the Nirvana unplugged version, inspired by The Vaselines, Jesus Wants Me for a Sunbeam, as the chapter unfolds.

"Your Mom was a giant spirit in a petite body, and she always thought that her heart was not very strong. The love and support from everyone who came forward at her death was evidence of how much she was loved, how much heart she had, and how much of it she gave." Taken from Pops' eulogy for Mom.

By June of 1997, Mary Jo had undoubtedly done her duty in raising her family to be good people. We think we are good, striving to put ego aside and positively contribute to this world. Each one of her children was independent with professional occupations. She had done very well in that regard, but heaven was coming to take her. Mom passed away on June 4, 1997. Her body took in its last breath in the presence of Dad, my brothers Balboa and Turk.

The outpouring of support for the family after her death was tremendous, and we all had to rally together as it would not be easy to put Mom in the ground and move forward. I grabbed Brother Spud and went shopping for a wiffle ball and bat. For some reason, there was a need to go outside and play in the yard. Our family was devastated. Getting together, we talked and shared stories about her greatness, and as we went back in time, we turned into little kids again, playing wiffle ball, shooting hoops, looking at a lot of pictures, laughing and crying and drinking beer, bourbon, more beer, anything to be found and cried some more. And then our friends and family came over and joined us drinking Pops' beer and laughing and crying.

Mom had taken no medications in the days before her passing. It was the assistance of hospice and a touch of morphine that sent her body over the edge while her spirit hung on to say goodbye. Mom never fully regained consciousness from the first dose in the afternoon, taking her last breath after midnight. Dad greatly regretted this and wanted everyone to know, "Never wait until the last day to say what you want. There was so much more I had held in and wished I had taken the time to tell your mother," It is rare for Pops to let his emotions show, "Your mother lived the way she wanted to live, right up to the very end."

For some reason, Dad felt the need to clarify something after reading an early draft of this memoir. "At the time of her passing, Turk was not in the room yet, but on the stairs on his way up to her room." Whatever, Dad, respectfully, I thought, because that was close enough for me, I felt it miles away in Utah and woke up bawling in my bed at 4 am. When the phone rang, I knew what he would say, and I packed a bag and flew home that morning.

The two brothers present at her death were also the first to report back that Mom had come forward to them in a dream very soon after her passing and before we even put her into the ground at Fern Hill Cemetery. The Holy Spirit was influential in Mary Jo and still is. The force is with her. This was turning into a KCGB, heebie-jeebies kind of story, only now it was the Mom-jeebies with her spirit hanging around for a while.

Turk's dream came to him the first evening after she passed. He became conscious within the dream and realized it was Mom standing in the back of the church at her upcoming funeral. Turk asked her out loud, "Mom, is that you?" She nodded as if she could hear him. Turk asked, "Can anyone else see you?" Mom looked at her James Ronald and said, "Only if they believe." My brother remembers her image to this day. Now I was happy for him to get a message from Mom so quickly, but also disappointed as I had thrown a mattress down on the floor in her library the night after her death and said, "Come and get me, Mom, let's talk." I slept in her library, on the floor, the entire week I was home. Nothing. We had been speaking a lot about life, and we were overdue for a follow-up talk with a revised lesson plan. Maybe she was saving that up for a later date, but I wanted to hear from her. My soul must not have been ready, or as I have learned, you can't force it.

Balboa reported a similar dream experience when Mom appeared to him while he was asleep. His version is a little different because he saw other people in the room and not just Mom, describing the family standing around and arguing about something, and when he looked around, he could see Mom watching. She looked back at her little Terence Dominic and gave him the Mom Smile that radiated love and warmth. That smile hit him like St. Elmo's Fire, which occurs when the atmosphere becomes charged, and plasma is created between an object and the air around it. When Balboa felt that jolt, Mom gave him a reassuring nod, telling him that "everything was going to be all right" about the arguing.

Joy Scout Maria has strong memories of dreams but initially does not walk away with happy emotions. Mom would come to her while sleeping, "We would just be together, snuggling and talking, but then each time, she had to go as if the cancer were taking her away again and again. It broke my heart repeatedly each time she left" Tearfully, my sister described the terrible heartache she felt when requesting, "Please do not come back anymore because I have to keep reliving the pain of losing you." After a few honest breaths of emotion, Maria shared, "In the last 25 years, along the way, I would say there have been a few pop-ins, and in those times, I have come to feel better about her visits" while adding "for unexplainable reasons when I feel her warmth and visualize her mom smile, it is as if I feel her presence, especially when I am performing and hitting my groove."

Mom did not come to me in a dream until years later. But she did come to me when the family argued about what outfit to bury their mother in. I was not fully processing what was happening when picking clothes to bury Mom. After the fact, I felt she was there to help me find the right outfit because my brothers were picking out shit. As I walked into her bedroom, made my way around the mahogany makeup stand, and looked at the five recommendations of clothes being laid out, I was still waiting for the 70s polyester, floral, dated dresses to call out to me. If Mom were watching, she would have been in agony.

She must have been because I was directed to the closet in the red room, left of the bathroom, which used to be Balboa's room. When Balboa enlisted in the United States Army, she used this closet for overflow, or maybe it was her New Age closet because the big closet in her bedroom was full of old-age stuff. And there it was, a light blue vest with pink carnations that she wore layered over a pink shirt, exactly how it was hung on the hanger. She would have worn this with denim jeans, a skirt, or skorts. This was it. I returned it to the bedroom and put it on the bed with the others. My choice did not get a glowing look of approval from my brothers. They were being donkeys. Some women from Pop's work brought over a pile of grub for us, and he invited them upstairs to see if they could give an opinion. They agreed with my selection. I tried to tell them that it was meant to be.

Soon after the wardrobe selection, we looked through pictures to put on display for the celebration of life when I found the perfect one that captured the essence of her spirit. In the photo, Mom is smiling, and a sunbeam shines down on her face. Her right hand is resting just under her ear, the look on her face is radiant, and that is when it hit me. Boom. This image is perfect for the order of service. Mom is wearing the exact outfit I found in the new-age closet. The only thing that needed to be added was the Taize cross she wore religiously. We found the Taize cross and, for bonus points, the earrings she was wearing in the picture. Our Mom truly loved the

Taize Community in France and its principles of reconciliation and welcoming all denominations. The music of Taize is simple and beautiful. She put it together for us in Aberdeen, bringing it home with her after selling a few shares of Starbucks to fund her latest trip to France. It was only fitting that she had her Taize cross.

Even in death, our Mom faced a final conflict with her church. If a Catholic Priest were to perform the service of Mass at her funeral, they would be unable or unwilling to offer the sacrament of communion to those who were not Catholic, including reverends and ministers of other denominations. The hypocrisy, Mary Jo must have thought. Dad was direct and surly when he said, "This was intolerable for your mother as she would expect all followers to be welcome to accept the Body of Christ." Father Alfred worked up a solution that was in agreement with Pops. I turned to him and asked, "You mean a loophole?" He gave me the look of disgust, which I had seen before, and rephrased. "Your Brother Alfred did have a brilliant mind Pops." Yes, he did. Father Alfred dedicated her Requiem Mass with Sacrament the evening before her memorial and graveside service.

When we were at the cemetery for the final moments of her burial, I tried to be strong and told myself with borrowed words from Chief Joseph of the Nez Perce upon his surrender to U.S. Troops, "From where the sun now stands, I will fight no more forever." I substituted the word cry for fight. "I will cry no more forever" was a motto that lasted for about an hour. In the year 1904, Chief Joseph died, according to his doctor, of a broken heart. We could all say we left a part of our hearts on the hill at Fern Hill Cemetery as we put our mother into the ground. As I looked down towards the panorama of Grays Harbor, it was tough to let go and accept her essence was gone, but I did recognize that her body lay in rest with a good view of the Chehalis River and a couple of stone's throw away from the "Muddy Banks of the Wishkah." Yet still, she was gone, and we all missed her.

At the celebration of life gathering at our house, a picture was taken of her grandchild Nicholas at not quite three years old while sitting on the lap of Haley Montana, named after the comet and the great state. Haley is the granddaughter to Aunty and the daughter of cousin Mary. There was a bobbing of the head, slowly dozing off until finally hitting the snooze button and falling asleep. Nicholas was out cold. Behind them is a woman in a yellow dress playing the violin. The woman playing the violin would become essential to our lives as we gathered and moved forward as a family. But before we could, death came calling again. God was not done challenging our family. Really God?

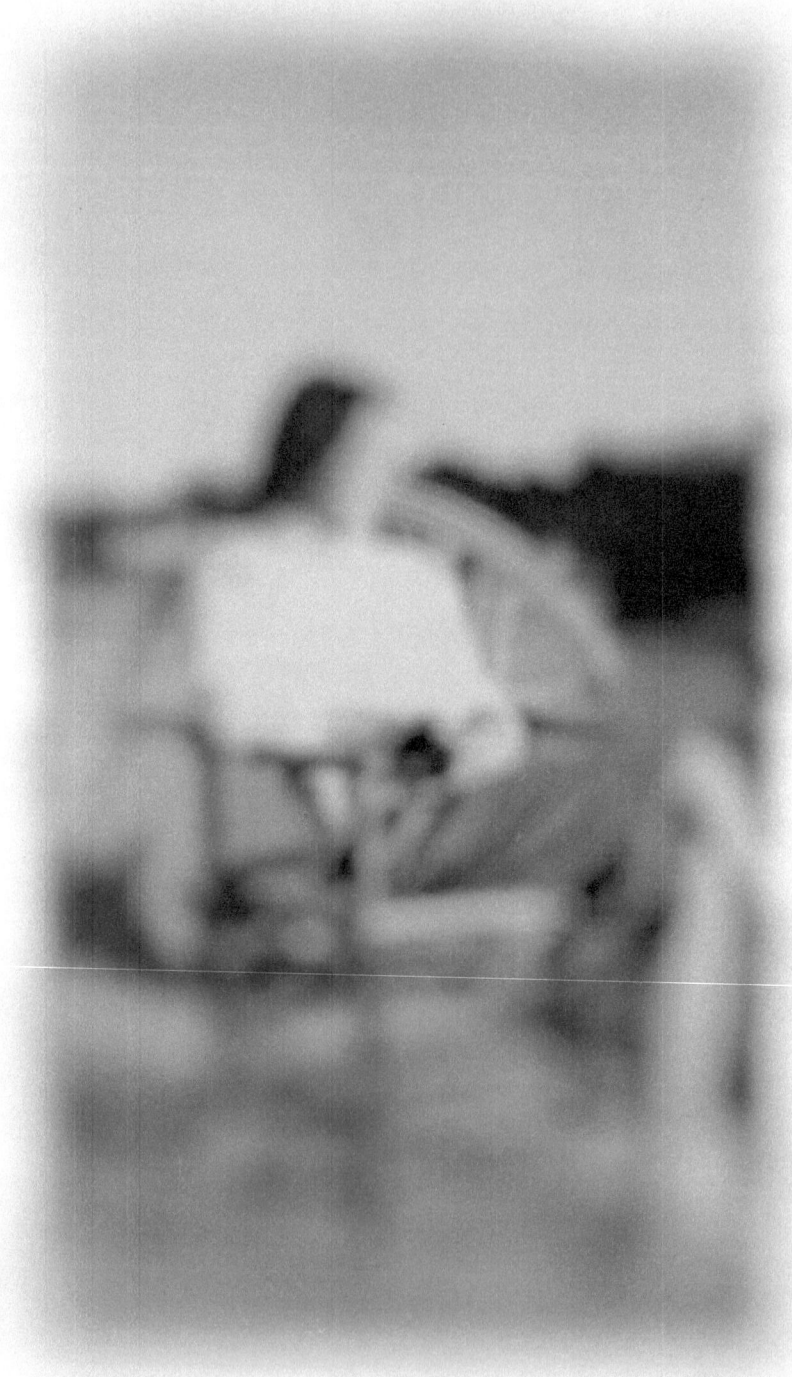

Chapter Fifteen

Moving on without Mom

Star Date: 1998 - 2002

I was furious with God for taking our mom from us at 61. In the last decade, we have gotten on the same page. Gone were the anarchy of the past and the lack of Mom time I longed for growing up. We became really good friends, and I could get as much time with her as my schedule allowed, so it was always a special time when we were together. Her books and our conversations were the driving force behind helping me grow. ***Damn it***, I must have muttered many times. She was getting going in her life and was truly special to all of us. How dare you, God. I was 32, and if you have ever lost a parent early in life, you get it, although the older I get, the more I understand it is not easy losing a parent at any age. Please know you are not alone. If you were to multiply my fury for Mom's passing and multiply that by 10,000, you would be a few degrees of heat away from what I felt when Dad called a year after Mom died.

"I have been diagnosed with advanced Colon and Prostate Cancer."

Now I was at a tipping point. *Damn it* — was replaced with *Fuck it* — Sorry God, but the Big Kahuna and I were headed for a showdown. Joy Scout put it to me this way when recalling Lieutenant Dan in Forrest Gump, when he climbs the mast of the shrimp boat Jenny in the middle of Hurricane Carmen and has it out with God. That's how I visualized myself, screaming into the gale force winds, "You will never sink this boat," while challenging God, "Is that all you got?" I wanted to be mad at God for a while longer. I did want to stay angry. I did my best work when I was furious—sometimes got more done that way. But anger can also have the opposite effect. Sometimes it is just not healthy to stay angry. I rode the storm out and settled my differences with God for now. Dad was going to need me. Dad was going to need all of us. I needed Dad, and Dad needed God. That put the three of us in the same boat. No way this one was going to sink.

Pops rallied back, just like you would expect, just as he had done after John Joseph had died. Like when St Joseph Hospital closed, he returned to school, earning his Master's from the University of Colorado at Denver. This rally would be a little harder for him, though; this time, it would take a lot of intestinal fortitude and grit. What's it going to be, Pops? He chose determination, telling me and all the world, "I will just dig it out of the dirt."

He always liked that phrase, sounding like Kenny Venturi, his favorite golfer of all time, one time driving to Canada so he could follow his every shot in person. Pops says, "If you want to get good, you must go to the driving range, grind away on your game, and dig it out of the dirt." That is precisely what he did. He had a chunk of his colon removed, and then a year later, the doctors took care of the issues with his prostate. His background in the medical field at the hospital helped him navigate his options. He was not taking this lightly and wanted to be as aggressive as possible based on the information at hand. We needed him to be bold, including radiation treatments and active surveillance. He then made sure his boys had check-ups starting at age 40. This was serious business, mind you. If doctor visits for colon and prostate were like a rock concert, we would all be groupies for Dr. Jelly Finger and The Butt Scopes. This advice saved my life. Sixteen polyps later, still no cancer. The Twins would also agree – It saved their life as well. I guess we, the little donkeys, have graduated from groupies to headliners. Get a butt scope.

Without Mom, the game of golf became our family passion. Thanks to Balboa, he created a trophy, so once a year, we decided to get together and have a family golf tournament. Pops was determined to return to the course to show his boys that old guys rule. He did, twice, even at 75, he whooped us and claimed the trophy. Our dad was the 2012 Donkey Open Champion. He almost shot his age, birdie on 15, lip out a birdie on 16, par on 17, charging home with a 79.

2012 Hulscher Open Pops 79, Old Timer 82, Joey 85, Balboa 90

Hole #	1	2	3	4	5	6	7	8	9	Out	Initial	10	11	12	13	14	15	16	17	18	In	Total
Blue Tees	369	405	144	419	570	119	321	390	148	2972		625	395	175	360	354	200	340	370	409	3412	6412
White Tees	350	395	120	389	532	110	315	460	130	2801		515	385	155	355	345	170	330	370	404	3029	5830
Men's Par	4	4	3	4	5	3	4	5	3	35		5	4	3	4	4	4	4			35	70
Men's Handicap	10	6	16	8	2	18	12	4	14			1	5	17	9	11	15	13	7	3		
Joe	25	14	25	13	26	23	14	25	25	40	Joe	16	18	5	25	5	24	25	24	25	45	85
Tim	25	25	24	24	6	34	4	6	23	41	Tim	25	25	14	25	25	24	25	14	24	41	82
Pop	25	16	3	25	26	3	13	36	12	34	Pop	37	24	35	24	5	12	14	24	25	40	79
Terry	26	15	25	26	17	13	26	26	14	47	Tim	17	25	2	24	14	13	14	24	36	42	90

Pops found love again when he met the violin player in the yellow dress. They were married, and she settled into living in the house on the hill. Her name is Asikainen (Sherry), and she is a retired schoolteacher who likes reading, puzzles, acting, and music. Sherry loves The Beatles and sharing her Finnish heritage. Packaged with the Asikainen deal came her two children, Taz (Mary) and Mani-Oh (John), aged 21 and 18, all becoming part of our tribe. Our sister Joy Scout was 25 at this time.

The boys needed to make it easier for Sherry. Our Mom had taken care of everything when we were home, cooking all the meals and making the arrangements. It was as if they expected their stepmother to be the same. But she wasn't. Of course. I asked Sherry to describe the culture of joining our family when she held her thoughts for a second, maybe more than a second, as she gathered her words. "I believe in teaching a man to fish, never believing it was my job to wait on a man."

Sherry understood Mary Jo may have done so, applying no fault, but that would not be her role. I always appreciate her honesty, especially during one of our recent quiet nights together when Sherry told me she attended school with Kurt's parents in the 60s. This immediately got my attention. "Tell me more" She described his mother, Wendy, as quiet and with a lovely singing voice. She was part of the school choir. Sherry would be well positioned to make these observations, as she was part of the school orchestra. As for Kurt's father, Donald would wisecrack at her asking, "What ya got in there?" as she passed him carrying her violin case as she boarded the school bus from the south side of Aberdeen.

Family porch photo 2004

Ghost in the Attic

KCGB

Act Two
The Boy From the Porch

A Memoir

Joseph Hulscher

Chapter Sixteen

Wake Up Call

Star Date: 2002 - Current Date

In 2002 and five years after her death, Mom rang the chapel bell in the attic of the Old Timer, just as she had with Father Stohr. It was time to wake him up. My brother had filed away what Mom told him that day when she stopped by his office the month before dying. He thought it might be important later, and now later was here. Buying the Nirvana CD was his wake-up call. It was a spine-tingling Holy Shit moment when Old Timer recalled what Mom shared five years ago, almost to the day. As his memories of their lunch date returned, so did the events of 1986 and the three times that summer he had interactions with the Boy From the Porch, the boy Mom was talking about. By his admission, Old Timer was way behind the times when it came to Kurt and his band, and 2002 would be his first real listen to the famous music kid from our hometown. I question if my brother even knew Kurt played the guitar left-handed before listening to the CD and learning about the band.

On the other hand, Brother Spud was an early fan of the band. He'd been cruising in his buddy's car when he first heard a cassette of Bleach. For all he could recall, he had never met Kurt ever in his life. I distinctly remember when Spud called me in the fall of 1991 and told me about this new band Nirvana and to watch for the Smells Like Teen Spirit video getting heavy rotation on M-TV.

Who is Nirvana? I asked. He was amped up. "Novoselic and Cobain." I was stumped, "who is Cobain?" I met Chris (Krist) in 9th grade when he moved to Aberdeen from California; I even remember asking him if he played basketball. "Bummer," I thought when he said he was into soccer. Based on Krist's height, he must have been asked that a lot. That dude was tall, a funny outcast, and wore straight-leg levis. We wore flares. I had never heard of the other kid, even checking the yearbooks. No photos. Who was this Kurt Donald Cobain, frontman of the band Nirvana?

When Old Timer connected with Spud, he was surprised to learn his little brother experienced a similar visit with Mom five years ago. They began sharing information, primarily by email, because one lived in Arizona and the other in Olympia. These and other conversations with the family brought back more memories, and the story grew. Over the next few years, there were general conversations and much doubt. Things took off in 2007 when Old Timer, Spud, and brother Joey all happened to purchase the extensive "Nirvana — The Biography" by Everett True, all at the same time, but in different cities without discussion. The first 39 pages centered around Kurt's life in Aberdeen, much of which we did not know. This gave us a roadmap to follow.

When visiting Pops at home, we also passed around Charles Cross's 2002 biography of Kurt, "Heavier than Heaven," which Sherry had purchased and left sitting around for us. The more we talked and researched, the more we narrowed the time to the summer of 1986. But was it Kurt? Could it have been him? It fits with the time he'd been couch surfing, and brother Spud confirmed the year when he remembered that was the summer Mom made him get a job at Safeway. Old Timer remembered I was on crutches and something about a red guitar, the kid-sized one Balboa got for Christmas years back. By now, I had to know more and started to journal the stories my brothers were sharing with me. I am glad I did. There were notes we all had forgotten. See the photo of Balboa on page 49.

In the summer of 2011, I interviewed Old Timer for a full rundown of this growing family legend. I lucked out and caught him on a morning before he had to head to the airport back to Arizona. Until then, Spud was an open book in our talks, while his brother had kept it close to the vest. He began with Mom showing up for lunch when she should have been home in bed and filled in what he could remember. Old Timer thought Kurt might have been sleeping in the basement. That was a pretty big scoop. We even brought Pops into the mix and asked if he knew anything about this. "Did you find him in the basement and kick him out?" Nothing from Pops except, "Huey the dog would have known." This was our legend for a few years, thinking Pops must have found Kurt in the basement, given him the boot, and wasn't talking. Huey, the watchdog, is his story, and he is sticking to it. A story that has never changed in two decades of asking.

Old Timer and I hooked up again when the pandemic hit. This was when it happened to me. Mom rang my bell. I was scrolling my Facebook feed when an old 8mm video started to play. I posted this years ago for Brother Turk, a throwback to him playing Nerf hoops in the McKinley house. I could hear Mom speaking in the background. The only thing was, this was a silent video. She said, "Your eyes are open now," repeating the phrase. "Oh look, your eyes are open now," I asked my girlfriend, Penny Jo. "Are you hearing this?" She was.

Just a few days before, I had assisted her father, known as Fred, cross over in death. I was with him through the final weeks of his life, administering the morphine as instructed by the hospice nurse. In his last year, Fred became my friend. As his mind and body neared the end, it felt like Mom was with me the entire time, keeping me grounded in the moment while comforting the family. The hospice nurse cleared the room. I was the only one there. I kissed his forehead and said you can go now. And he did. Shortly after.

With that, I fully understood her call to ministry; I got it, Mom, how the Church robbed you of your calling, and it took me back to your death, how I was not present and unable to be with you when you passed away. I felt it with Fred. You were there with me. So that is what you meant when you told me, "Your eyes are open now." You bet they were. The Mom jeebies were back, but in a good way, and now, I was the one who wanted answers. Where are my notebooks? I went to see my brothers Old Timer and Spud, just like Mom did in 1997.

Pops always intended to write a book about Mom, so this gave us a chance to work together. Talk about a mentor. You have read the story of My Dying Mom and Kurt Cobain. We're sharing the origins of the story. The story of "The Boy From the Porch." This is what we had to start with. This is what the brothers Old Timer and Spud were able to put together as I grilled them for information. As much as we can remember, anyway. Join me. Let's take a trip. We will target the summer of 1986, precisely Grays Harbor and the town of Aberdeen, Washington. It is time to meet the Boy from the Porch before he becomes Kurt Cobain, the legend, and his actual image is hijacked. This story is not a legend. This story is the truth.

Mood Enhancer: I recommend you cue up the song "I Can't Shake It," the 1998 Melvins' version. It will give you the beat we're looking for to start this scene. When the story got ahold of me, that was how I felt, and I could not shake it.

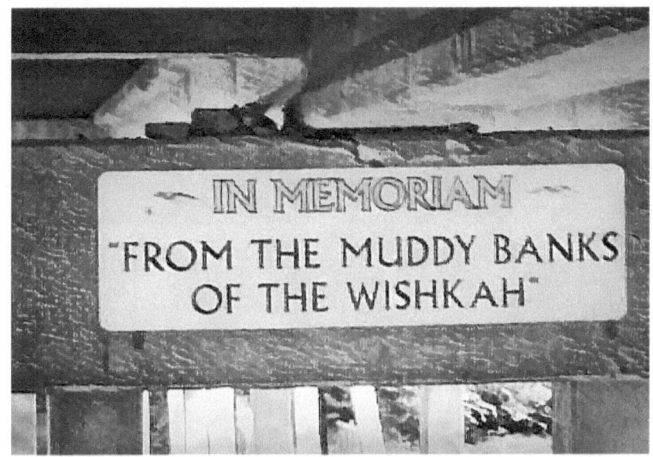

Kurt Cobain Landing -- Save Kurt's Bridge

Chapter Seventeen

Boy from the Porch

Star Date: 1986 - 1988

"Hey Johnny, Ya Got Any Pot?"

"Ya, I got a little morsel that might be enough for us to get baked."

Johnny's friend, Nyquil from baseball, was on the phone, and they agreed to meet at the end of the alley that was the driveway to our neighbor Todd's house. He may not have liked it back then when I called him Waldo. Sorry, Todd. Conveniently, an opening at the end of our fence would make for a most excellent and discrete exit and entrance. Johnny thought it would only be one guy, so his heart sank when he saw three walking toward him. He was down to his last bud, one little morsel, and no green cross stores in 1986. He was happy to share it with a friend, but now it would be split four ways. You did not want to be last in the line on that exchange. No way. The last in line very well was going to be sucking ash.

Nyquil introduced Johnny to Kurt and a third person, yet to be determined, but we think it was Bodhi. They passed the neighbors' chain link fence as they got near the backyard. Its job was to contain two German Shepherds. Fortunately, they were nowhere to be seen. When you lost a ball in their yard, it was gone for good unless the dogs were inside the house. You knew they were inside the house because if they saw you enter their yard, the dogs would shred the kitchen curtains, trying to get you. This was the home of Rudy, the former band director from the school. His students thought so much of him that one year they stole his front porch, well, the steps to his front porch. That may have been why he owned those dogs. His marching bands were legendary and award-winning. RIP neighbor.

Johnny walked them along the clothesline path where when we weren't home, we chained our dog, a Husky Lab furball mix called Huey, named after Hugh Anthony Cregg III, otherwise known professionally as Huey Lewis and the News.

They approached the porch when Kurt said, "We don't need to go inside your house. We can smoke outside."

"No, it's all right," Johnny said. "My parents aren't home."

They walked through the kitchen and into the front parlor. A right turn and they were walking up the stairs. "You've got a nice house," Kurt told Johnny. "Whatever," Johnny said, slightly uncomfortable with people thinking we might be better than someone just because we had a big house. He knew we weren't rich, and he lived in his brother's hand-me-downs. At the top of the stairs, they hung another right and went into Johnny's blue and gold room – the colors of our high school that Dad and I had painted before handing the space over to Spud after my senior year. This was a special room where people could hang out, listen to music and play video games.

When they entered the room, Nyquil pointed towards Kurt and told Johnny, "He's in a band, and they're really good. Like Metallica, good. Not in the Metallica style, but just as forceful and impressive."

"Yeah, you're gonna see me on MTV one day," Kurt said. "No, no, not MTV, more like Saturday Night Live." Johnny laughed a little and wondered who Nyquil's friend thought he was. This was in 1986 in Aberdeen. Johnny then shifted into this super positive persona that he could do on command. The family was familiar with this Johnny. A little like McConaughey, but we called him Spud. He had a unique strut coined the *spud walk*. At the same time, he would make a clicking noise with his mouth, snap his fingers and point his index fingers at you, and fire off a wisecrack. Johnny was in full-blown spud mode when he told Kurt, "You can do anything you want to. You can do anything you put your mind to." This was what Mom taught us, and Johnny believed her.

"You could be a doctor or a lawyer or anything. Well, not a doctor or lawyer, you know what I mean. Maybe not doctors or lawyers because they were sellouts, and stoners like us are not sellouts." Kurt was amused by his ramblings when he said, "It's dusty in here," Johnny wasn't home much and not really into dusting and did not care if he lived in a dusty dump.

Before Johnny could answer, Kurt said, "Well, entertain us. We're your guests. Entertain us!"

Johnny was thrown. He hadn't even invited this guy over, wasn't used to entertaining people, and tended to go to other people's houses. He showed them posters, a baseball, and other stuff before Bodhi saved him from his rambling anxiety with, "Okay, dude, where's the weed?" Johnny pulled out his little morsel and told them that was all he had and hoped they could get stoned off it. Nyquil suggested they go outside to smoke, but since no one was home, Johnny thought he was noble when he said they could blow it out the window. They were super jacked when he produced a pipe from his desk made out of a toilet paper roll and tin foil, at which Kurt laughed and said, "What the hell is this?"

"A poor man's glass pipe," Johnny said.

The foil was used to create the bowl you cut from the toilet paper roll. You cover the end of the roll with your hand while you take the hit and remove it to un-carb the chamber and release the last of the smoke. Johnny took the first toke. They had to pass it quickly, and each could only take one puff. They then attempted to blow the smoke out the bedroom window, but the windowsill had been painted over so many times it would only open a little. They had to get down on their knees to take the hit so the smoke could escape out the bottom of the window.

They were starting to get mildly stoned when Bodhi said to Johnny. "Hey, didn't you used to go out with that Michelle girl?" He nodded. "She's not a little girl anymore, is she?" Little brother had just broken up with her after one of his friends told him she was cheating. He heard she was with a guy out of high school who was into cocaine, so he wasn't really in the mood to talk about her. "Shut the fuck up, man," Nyquil told Bodhi.

Kurt started to pitch Johnny a little shit about his jock posters on the wall. There may have been Michael Jordan, Herschel Walker, and a picture of Billy Simms from the Detroit Lions. Nyquil pitched shit back at Kurt, protecting his friend. They laughed as they headed back down the stairs, through the kitchen, and returned to the back porch. Kurt and Bodhi were standing below the patio in the grass when Old Timer walked out the back door. He is usually quiet and reserved, so it was out of the norm for him to say, as he did, "How is ya doing, fellas?" I guess he was trying to be a little more social as his twin, Balboa, his best friend, was stationed in Germany with the Army. They all started talking and figured out that Old Timer and Kurt had been in the same class year in high school before Kurt dropped out.

Kurt said he was looking for a place to stay as he was bunking with one of Nyquil's twin brothers. Old Timer offered, "If anything, you can sleep in our basement," showing Kurt how to bust in via the left stairwell. At the bottom of the stairs was a door that would slide on a rail track, like a barn door. It was held closed by a 1 x 4 board that could be wedged against the door to keep it from rolling open. If you leaned into the door with your shoulder or bumped it with your hip, the board dropped, and you could enter the house. There was a ghetto toilet down there. It looked like an outhouse, and we used it if we were in a hurry when playing in the yard. Kurt nodded and said, "Okay," then returned to the porch. Johnny thought the Old Timer was losing it and being a dumb shit.

We don't even know this person, and he's telling him he can sleep in the basement?

Kurt had picked up an old kid-sized guitar, the red one Balboa had left behind in the basement, and took an interest in it, saying it was perfect for strumming and portable. "Do you think I could have it?" he asked. But Old Timer said it was Balboa's, so he couldn't just give it away. He started to fiddle with the strings, which worried Old Timer. Mom had a baby grand, and the blind guy Fletcher, who came to tune it, had accidentally scratched it once. Mom liked the tuning but had been upset with the scratch. Kurt seemed to know what he was doing, and it wasn't long before he'd rearranged the strings and played the kids' guitar left-handed.

"That's good," Old Timer told him. "That could be Top 40." He instantly regretted it. "Fuck Top 40," Kurt said. His tone was harsh, and there was an extended hiatus in group discussion. It was how he responded that startled the Old Timer. He recognized how Kurt had registered a highly emotional response for just a three-word phrase. There was something in how he said it, and Old Timer noted this when thinking, *he must be really serious about that top 40 shit.* Kurt nodded in response as if they understood each other and continued playing as though it was MTV Unplugged on the back porch. Still, Nyquil, who was younger and getting testy, eventually said, "Fuck, I'm not sitting around here all day listening to you play the guitar." A buzzkill was how Old Timer described Nyquil.

They took off, with Nyquil still on Kurt's case, telling him he needed to shower, pointing out his greasy hair, and pulling on his hat. They headed towards Sam Benn Park, and Johnny suggested,

"Let's get some alcohol."

"You got any money?" the boys asked. But nobody had any money, so Johnny said, "Well, I could get some change from my brother's dresser or dad's drawer."

"How are we going to get the alcohol?" Johnny had the perfect solution. "We can take the wagon and find my brother."

The wagon was the Chevy Kingswood Lime Green Beauty that was now 15 years old and had been passed down from its original use as the Family Truckster driven by Mom Queen of the Carpool to Turk driving us to the lake, and then the Meat Man (my best friend) put the first dent in it. The Twins gave it to Johnny to drive until the back window leaked so bad that stale and infested water sloshed around in the back. Nathan and Sideline Auto Wrecking was the next investor in line for the luxury cruiser, where glorious parts pullers exfoliated it into scrap metal in return to earth.

"I don't want to get any alcohol," Nyquil said, causing Johnny and Kurt to exchange glances. They kept walking, coming across some of the oldest local homes built with highfalutin timber aristocracy monies at the turn of the century. Kurt started to murmur, repeating, "This is out of our range, this is out of our range, man, out of our range, out of our range, man."

"What the hell are you talking about?" Nyquil said.

"Like ranges on a map, man, you know how there are different ranges on the map? On a map, this is out of our range." He turned to Johnny. "Man, I am stoned off that one hit."

Johnny was bummed they would not get alcohol and wanted to leave the group. He didn't fancy going walkabout, but at the same time did not want to insult them. Ultimately, he said, "Hey, do you guys mind if I leave?" They were good with it. Everyone went in a different direction when he turned around and heard Kurt mumble about writing a song about this. Spud headed for home, also feeling the effects of that one hit.

Back at Pilgrim Heights, Mom had arrived home, pulling into the carport near where the boys had been standing. When she walked through the back door into the kitchen, boom, the universal smell of skunk, the same odor she had learned about 15 years earlier attending the Satsop Rock Festival in 1971. Following her nose, she pinpointed the source to the blue and gold room. Within moments, Johnny walked through the door, and by the time he got upstairs, he found himself face-to-face with Mom. No doubt she had her hands firmly on her hips.

"I can smell marijuana," she told him. "You have been smoking marijuana in your room. I can smell it." Johnny denied it, but Mom persisted. "I saw you were walking down the street with those hooligans," she continued. "I want you to get a job. I hear that Safeway is hiring, and I want you to go down there tomorrow and apply." He tried to open his mouth, but before he could put the words together, Mom uncorked the look that all moms have, the one from the semi-circle, and there was not much more Johnny could do. The next day he went down to Safeway and was hired to bag groceries. To this day, Johnny blames those hooligans for his

Mom forcing him to get a job. He has never forgotten how terrified he was, sitting in the manager's office, not knowing what to say.

As it was, Johnny could have listened to Kurt or his friend Nyquil when they suggested smoking outside, maybe even behind the garage, huh, Spud? Hindsight is 20/20; without Spud's poor judgment, we wouldn't have this story. Somehow, the Old Timer skated out of this scenario without Mom giving him a shake-down.

And just like that, life moved forward until Kurt returned a few days later. Before that can happen, though, Spud has a theory he would like to share with you.

It has to do with the song Negative Creep.

The truth is, there is no way I could make this shit up!

From 2002 to the present day, Johnny has remembered more and more. With these details, he developed a very valid opinion that the song "Negative Creep" from the album Bleach may have been associated with the events of that day. At first, I may have thought his opinion didn't hold water and may have told him he was full of shit, and I did. He would reply audibly and in sign language, using the middle finger. This happened more than once, not often, but over quite a few years.

Songwriters pull ideas from several places and experiences. It becomes personal to the listener, and they can own the subjective meaning based on their ear and interpretation. Dave Grohl explained it better than the pile of shit I was trying to sell my brother. "That's one of the great things about music. You can sing a song to 85,000 people, and they will sing it back to you for 85,000 different reasons."

Spud thinks that in Negative Creep, Kurt is singing about him and his experience with the girlfriend who dumped him for the cocaine guy. He and a friend had the Bleach cassette on repeat. He didn't know the band was from our hometown at first, but when he did, this made it interesting to him. The published lyric sheet online shows the verse in question to be Daddy's Little Girl, but back then, lyrics were not printed with the cassette jacket. The truth is everyone makes up their lyrics from time to time. Singing in the car on a solo drive? I always make up words. My brother thought he heard "Johnny's Little Girl." He understood she was not a little girl anymore.

Years later, I came across the claimed first recording of Negative Creep on YouTube. Search — Negative Creep. First Live Performance 02/25/89. East Ballroom, Seattle, WA. — You'll be able to find the clip and listen. What do you hear? A "J" for Johnny or a "D" for Daddy? (I have found the Fender Jaguar upload version of the song to have the best audio)

I had to chalk one up for Brother Spud on this one. I could hear "J." I was hearing Johnny. I am hearing Johnny. It sounds to me like Kurt singing Johnny. Spud was not full of shit. It is as if Kurt is playing around with both the D and the J sometimes to find his comfort in performing the song, being the first live performance for the band. The third verse stanza comes around, and Kurt sells it. "Johnny." Spud was not full of shit. I love you, brother. This is very special to our family and maybe friends of Kurt who know his truth from back then. He could sing whatever he felt like that day, and the lyrics did not hold special meaning to Kurt when writing, except maybe this one time.

I want you to know I'm confident in my firsthand view. *Negative Creep* – The Boy from the Porch Edition was written by our friend Kurt (duh) and is based on his experience of getting baked with Spud – *and I'm stoned* - and deciding to go walkabout on the street with no name. Admiring houses that were *out of our range* that inspired this one and only version.

We believe Kurt is singing *Johnny's Little Girl*.

Respectfully, put that in your toilet paper roll pipe and smoke it. Just be sure to blow it out the window, or you could run the risk of having to get a job bagging groceries at Safeway. For note: In 1993, Kurt told Spin Magazine that he "didn't give a flying fuck what the lyrics were about" when he wrote songs for the first album. In one of his first interviews, he also told Sounds Magazine that many of the lyrics on the album were inspired by his life in his hometown.

Another element that is often overlooked is that it was just a short time later, in January of 1988, when Kurt, Krist Novoselic, and Dale Crover, also known that day as Ted, Ed, and Fred, laid down a 9 1/2 track demo that would later be passed on to Sub Pop. Ted, Ed, and Fred played the same set that night in Tacoma at the Community World Theatre before the super sub drummer Dale headed off to Frisco to rejoin Buzz Osborne of Melvins. Buzz and Dale were close friends of Kurt and Krist. That would mean Kurt's songs written before January of 1988 would greatly be influenced by his years earlier on the Harbor.

For historians and those of you fact-checker, Negative Creep was not one of the 9 ½ songs demoed that day. It also meant that Kurdt and Krist would again find themselves seeking a drummer. A classified ad was placed in Rocket Magazine.

> "DRUMMER WANTED. Hard, heavy, to hell with your 'looks and hair a must.' Soundgarden, Zep, Scratch Acid. Kurdt 352-0992."

Constable Huey reporting for duty.

A few days after Johnny started work at Safeway, Kurt returned
to our house and knocked on the door. The oracle answered, our
Mom. He asked if he could speak with her son. Mom went inside
and tapped the Old Timer on the shoulder.

"There's a boy here to see you."

Old Timer went to the door and saw it was the guy he had met a
few days ago. They stood on the porch for a minute, then Kurt said,
"I need a place to stay." Old Timer wanted to do the right thing,
but being a good guy, he asked our mom first. She said she would
need to meet the boy. This was at a point in time when Mom had
become very wise, when her tuning fork was lit like an Olympic
flame, and you could not bullshit her. Kurt was invited into the

house and asked to sit with Mom in the kitchen. Old Timer stood out in the parlor area and kept his distance. She looked Kurt in the eyes and asked him,

"How is it that you have gotten yourself to not be with your family?" He described his parents' divorce and poor experiences of late with his mom.

"And what about your father?" — "I can't go back to live with my dad," he said, shaking his head.

Mom reflected on her father and how she forgave him in his final years when he was no longer drinking. Instinctively she activated her Mom smile, creating warmth – and softened her voice while holding his gaze to make her point.

"You must find a way to reconcile with your family at some point."

According to Old Timer, who was eavesdropping, this was the first time he recognized Mom's abilities as a counselor and healer, where she had moved past the role of YMCA director.

Mom continued speaking to Kurt, asking, "Do you do any drugs?" Kurt owned right up to it and answered,

"Yes, mam," pausing for a second, "Yes, mam, I do a little pot."

Mom appreciated his honesty, which went a long way with her. Still, she had reservations about having a stranger in the house with a daughter there and being unable to contact Pops to ask for his opinion. She felt guilty when telling him no – it went against her kind and compassionate nature and went to say to Old Timer it was bothering her. Joy Scout remembers Mom speaking of her guilt at being unable to help this boy, changing her mind but instructing Old Timer not to tell Dad. Meanwhile, he had already acted, telling Kurt to come back in an hour and to sneak in, giving directions to the shortcut to Finch Park. "You can take a drop-down path underneath the 6th Street bridge and onto Canyon Court."

Mom was thinking about how she could make him comfortable when Old Timer took honesty as the best policy approach and shared he had already given the okay to sneak in. Once again, the chosen one avoided getting into trouble. A blanket and a pillow, appeared from Mom when heading to the basement as instructed, finding Kurt below the stairwell, seeing him when his head popped out. The creaky door made it easy to get wind if someone were coming down the stairs. As far as we knew, Kurt spent the night and was gone in the morning.

Dad argues to this day Constable Huey (the watchdog) would have gone nuts if someone had been in the basement. I disagreed with Dad. We talked to Huey like he was part of the family, a regular Joe. Well, I did. We might have been high, but they were everyday conversations, so once Huey got to know you, he would be likelier to wiggle his tail, lick your face and keep you warm than he was to bark when he smelled you coming. We all agree that darn dog would sit on the back porch and bark at nothing some nights.

Old Timer said he did not think Kurt stayed again except that cigarette butts were found in the basement later that summer. Mom said she could smell cigarette smoke and asked if any of the boys had started smoking. Johnny remembers her asking and her following it up a few days later. He did not get the same benefit of the doubt as his brother Old Timer, answering for the third time, "No, Mom, I have not been smoking in the basement," when she said, "Forget it, I think we had a bum sleeping in the basement, your Dad found cigarette butts and a blanket." Full Stop. This did not make sense, like coming to a screeching halt. I need to cross-exam Pops and end the constable Huey story. Dad found what in the basement?

More importantly, Joy Scout reminded me of something else, Mom would never call someone a bum, so it got me thinking. Why would she say this, knowing it was the blanket given to Old Timer? Covering for Kurt? Covering for herself? This is when I figured it out and put all the pieces together. I never realized this before. Old Timer, Mom, and Spud were all on different frequencies. For one, Mom never told Dad. He verified this and passed the buck onto Huey. Secondly, she said bum to Johnny because Mom hadn't connected him with Kurt – she hadn't realized Kurt was one of the hooligans smoking pot with Johnny a few days before. Old Timer was quiet as instructed, so Johnny didn't know Kurt had returned to talk with his brother, let alone he was given a seat at the table and a meeting with Mom and the green light to spend the night.

Except for this one night, when he was coming home from somewhere, it could have been anywhere, and he took a leak in the Ghetto Toilet before going upstairs into the house. He remembers thinking that he heard someone say,

"Geez!"

It was a long and lengthy piss, his head leaning against the wall, sixteen, drunk on a cheap buzz, maybe Schmidt Ducks Animal Beer, and was letting it out after holding it in when he thought he heard things.

Dad is going to sell the house someday. With that ghetto toilet in the basement, it will be worth a gazillion dollars.

Introducing Ghetto Toilet

Couch surfing in the summer of 1986 was when Kurt came knocking on the door at the house on the hill. Archives from Everett True say this was when he borrowed money from his Mom to rent a shack at 1000 ½ East Second St in September of 1986. That puts us in the sweet spot of places he had slept, right between the Shillinger's couch and when he rented the shack. The Yellow Couch was a historical piece of Cobain legend donated to the Aberdeen Museum of History. Regrettably, it was then lost in a massive fire. Maybe we should present the Ghetto Toilet to the world when they rebuild the museum, and the people will line up for miles, headlights stretching out to the bluff! People will come, yes indeed. People will most definitely come to see the historical Kurt Cobain Memorial Outhouse.

It is unknown exactly when a friend of our family came to the house and asked the Old Timer if he wanted to go to a party, but we know it was after Kurt had slept in the basement. That friend needed someone to drive him around and someone who could help buy him a beer, both of which the Old Timer could do. Mayr lived a block away and attended school with us. We had known him since our youngest days. That kid could be an amusing character, and he could also cause a wee bit of trouble.

They fired up the Mercury Comet and turned the radio to 104.7 KDUX, the rock of the coast, and set out to my place to find some beer. I was bunking with my friend the Meat Man near Stewart Field and the Robert Gray Elementary School, helping him save money for his honeymoon while he helped me. I was on crutches, injured while turning a double play in slow pitch, and needed a place to stay without stairs. As Turk said, it was a bad beat, maybe even throwing a chair against the wall at the iconic Pourhouse Tavern when he heard the news of the injury diagnosis; it was torn ACL and MCL ligaments. Turk felt his brother's pain and knew it was a cheap shot to the knee that did him in. It was slow-pitch, after all.

I was of age, and Old Timer could rely on me to take care of their needs. To get beers, we would have gone to the 7-11 on B Street, where my crutches and I would contribute to the delinquency of a minor. On the Harbor, this was known as paying it forward like my brother before; if not my brother, someone else had a brother. Fortunately, Raj, Weedly, and Dunbar had an older sister. When it came to beer, we did not discriminate. Come to think of it, the same concept applied to weed. The other true-to-life legend in Aberdeen back then was that if you needed alcohol desperately enough, you could look for the fat man at the Morck Hotel, located on the same block as the liquor store. It only cost you a pint of whisky.

Having secured beer, Old Timer and Mayr headed towards the Wynooche, probably in the direction of property the Mayr Brothers' logging company owned. As it turned out, Mayr had duped Old Timer into driving out into the middle of nowhere, and by the time they got there, Mayr had drunk most of the beer. That was a party foul, and one of the reasons we say that kid could cause a wee bit of trouble. They backtracked towards town, taking the Wishkah Road before ending below the community hospital. It had now been a few hours from when their journey began. This is where Old Timer feels he may have merged two memories into one.

Maybe more than two, Mayr had done this before, even thinking the party may have been a year later, but admitting to the buying them beer part of the story as being true because that happened more than once. I would call them regulars on the weekend.

Regardless of when either memory found him at a party with Mayr around people, he did not know. My brother vividly recalled how the party-goers saw Mayr walk in the door and were either pissed off or surprised to see him. The atmosphere changed as if the air was sucked out of the room when a voice could be heard, "What are you doing here?" Mayr kept walking, oblivious to his abuse, Old Timer behind him, shutting the door, unsure if they were welcome when he made eye contact with the boy from the porch and immediately felt better; seeing someone he knew put him at ease.

Kurt's face lit up when he said, "Hey, I know you. You're the guy from the house up on the hill. You are that guy from that house up on the hill." Old Timer could tell when Kurt was genuine, like a real friend. And then he beamed, "I remember your Mom." Kurt was alive inside and appeared happy. He was listening to his recent demo and introduced Old Timer to his band.

A tall guy was lying, on the floor, maybe Sasquatch-like, and this long fellow talked about going to school with one of his brothers – me. This was clearly Krist Novoselic, but Old Timer was oblivious to the identity of the gent with long hair. Perhaps it was an early sighting of Chad Channing, who would fit the description. This is a tough one to validate because Old Timer never had a discussion with the gent with long hair, so that will be a mystery until I meet Krist again someday, and maybe we can triangulate coordinates and teleport ourselves back in time to answer that one when we land below Community Hospital.

Other people were moving about, but the setting was more of a private listening party, and Old Timer felt out of place. Kurt recognized this and turned to him and said about the demo, "Working on a new update, just giving it a listen." He then took a breath and said, "I don't think you will like it." Old Timer reported that most songs sounded heavy compared to current radio when Kurt hit fast forward and said to him, "Give this one a listen."

This song caught Old Timer's ear. It was less heavy, maybe even a bit more like the Beatles, but Old Timer remembered Kurt's comment from the porch, "Fuck Top 40," and decided to stay quiet and not poke the bear, only nodding in agreement. Kurt told Melody Maker, "When Bleach came out, I was very set in one frame of mind, except for that one song About a Girl. I had a few more like that I could've put on the album. And I wish I had because then it would've sounded more like Nevermind, and it wouldn't have been such a drastic leap." Old Timer told me he thought that one song, the Fuck Top 40 song, in reverse deja-vu type experience, sounded like the song "About a Girl."

Sitting around and getting comfortable, someone lit up a bowl when Kurt leaned into the Old Timer, telling him, "Your Mom was an extraordinary person in the way she talked with me. I liked how she walked me through the how and why she made her decision." He took a moment and continued, "It was direct, but she showed me respect. Right then, if I could choose, she would be the role model for all moms on how a mother could be."

The conversation in the kitchen had impacted him, making him reflect on his life. "I guess that makes us brothers, in a way."

The smell of doobage was in the air, and the pipe was getting so close to Old Timer that he could almost taste it. He reached out with excitement when the pipe was intercepted by Kurt, who looked at Tim and shook his head. — "Don't. Your mom would not approve." I imagined the Old Timer in the twilight zone of despair, close to the outer limits, as he sat there and watched smoke billow out of Kurt's mouth as he said, "Besides, you do not want to end up like us." Kurt knew what Mom would think and was being a good brother, one from another mother.

The truth is, if they were brothers, he might never have become a legend. Life might have been too easy. His tough times and family experiences fueled the angst and emotion from his earlier work. But then again, as kids, we were given a guitar, but no one embraced playing it. On the other hand, Kurt was given a guitar and ran with it. In just a few minutes on our porch, he picked up that same guitar, re-strung it so he could play it, and was putting on the show.

Kim Cobain described the impact of their parent's split in the *Montage of Heck* interview. Her brother felt ashamed and couldn't face his friends at school anymore because he wanted a typical family with a mother and father. Until now, Kim had the perfect brother, and their Mom, Wendy, had the perfect son. But then things changed for both of them. In countless interviews, Kurt agreed, sharing how much he desperately wanted the same thing, and in the end, we can all agree he needed the community that comes with family.

Later in Arizona, on the day of legalization in 2021, I interviewed the Old Timer on one of many occasions for this book. Having purchased a bottle of *Makers Mark* and some cannabis, I arrived and we got settled, making an offering in spirit with the whisky, when we realized we had a problem. We did not have a pipe. I first asked him if he had a pop can, but no aluminum cans could be found. A trip to the restroom revealed an empty toilet paper roll, and after the pillage of the kitchen, we found the foil and the tape we needed to make a friendly roundabout to this story—the return of the poor man's glass pipe.

~*~

When we lost our mom, we lost our world. For many of you close to Kurt, when you lost him, you lost your world. 1986 was a defining year. His compass was aligned when meeting our mother, giving him a look into the typical family he desperately wanted. In 1997, his Spirit returns to say thank you, or as Science would say, in her memories. We may never know which, but what we do know is this. Kurt Cobain passed through our life so quickly that we never even knew he was there, and, at that moment, he met greatness.

The greatness of **Mary Jo Hulscher – our Mom.**

Afterword

~*~

If you have made it this far, thank you for reading "The Boy From the Porch" and learning about our Mom. This topic was outside the main body of the memoir, but it deserves discussion. I always balanced any perceived "Spirit" message with the alternative view from a "Science" perspective. This is how I went about telling this story, by trying to balance multiple perspectives. I am my worst skeptic regarding Spirit energy, asking myself how I can debunk my own experiences. This is an excellent story for you to do the same and reflect on this theme while taking a journey back in time with me. I believe in writing this memoir, Mom does come back to me in Spirit and has continued to lend me small clues of direction to follow, just as she may have experienced with her visitor. Some private feelings led me to believe there was a message or two from Kurt, and my alter ego Science will tell you otherwise, so let's begin the debate.

Spirituality, or as I will call Spirit, is the life force that runs through us, and this lifeblood gives us existence and commonality with every human civilization on the planet. With that in mind, the

Spirit of Kurt Cobain came to visit Mom just three years after he took his own life. There was a compelling reason to explain the shared life force between Mom and Kurt, much like you would compare to the "Force" described in Star Wars but without the need to blow up a death star to make your point about its usefulness. It is more like Mom telling me to trust the force in how I receive spirit messages from her and others, trust my gut and feelings, and just run with it.

When Kurt returns to describe the investigator to Mom, he is wearing a sweatshirt with the name PRICK on it. That was no accident. I was searching for a Melvins' album to use and liked the word prick because Mom had met a few of those in her years. Great line. It wrote itself. After the fact, I checked Melvins-wiki to ensure the album was released before 1997, or else he could not wear it. It would be best to see why the album is named PRICK. I think Kurt was sending a message to Buzz and Dale. I had not learned the title's meaning when I chose that album name. Kurt acknowledged he got the message.

https://en.wikipedia.org/wiki/Prick_(Melvins_album)

In defense of Science, my opposing position is that in Mom's last few months, she began to recall several memories, including the brief interaction with the Boy from the Porch from eleven years earlier, back in the summer of 1986. At some point in her journey, she would take the leap and think this boy could be from the famous band from our hometown. This is where Science has a strong point. In the final months of Mom's life, it would have been impossible for her to have not seen, read, or heard about the rise and fall of the famous music kid from our hometown. April 1997 marked the third anniversary of Kurt's death. This timeline fits the sweet spot of when Mom would receive her spirit visits, and it would have been in the news everywhere.

Science tells us our brain can record all the information we see and hear without comprehending, such as when you drive across town, and it feels like you wake up and do not remember the last few miles. Imagine if every news story, headline, magazine cover, memorial, and falsehood associated with him would have been stored in the archive of her mind and available for recall once she made the connection. It took a while for her brain to find the correct hard drive file on the server, and these had to be backed up before Y2K and, most likely in 1986, backed up on a floppy disc. Once the connection was made, the recall began. Mom stuck a floppy in the Commodore 64 and brought the Boy from the Porch back to life in her mind. To her, it was not a figment of her imagination. We get that and very much appreciate her sharing her memories. Together they have woven a great story.

Suppose Spirit could have an opportunity to reply. That is a compelling argument, and I am there with you as this was not a figment of her imagination. If all you say is true, all I can ask is to think about this. If Mom was experiencing memory recall and, in the end, made the association that Kurt was the Boy from the Porch, why is it that she never once uses his name to either brother? She describes in detail every time he visits but never uses his name. Why? This is inconceivable considering that at the same time, the entire world knew his name. 30 years later, people still mourn his name. Ultimately, Mom still needs to receive the confirmation she sought when talking with Old Timer and Spud. Neither confirmed with her the visitor she was describing was Kurt Cobain. The other position concerns Mom asking my brother Johnny about a fire in California. That was not a Kurt Cobain story. That was specific to an event involving my brother that could not have occurred from memory recall and validated her visitor. How could Kurt have known about my brother's experience? Was he sending a warning? Put that in your poor man's pipe unless someone close to Kurt understands this fire message better than I do.

The reality is the reader gets to decide. I will have my opinion, and you will have yours. (Having both opinions improves my odds.) That is cool; that is how it should be so we can learn from each other. My first draft differs from the published version because of the universe's structure. If you put a question out there, the universe finds a way to send you the answer. We are all interconnected in some way. Pops, Marnie, Gibby, King, Old Timer, Spud, Dr. Fu, Running Wolf, and the endless number of neutrinos that pass through our bodies daily. I asked questions and learned from you. That is how we ended up with the story we have today.

Respectfully yours,

Brother Joey.

Author Thoughts

I never became comfortable trying to be Kurt's spokesperson, nor should I be. I once picked up his journals in a bookstore, opened them, and something made me shut them and put it down. It felt like an intrusion of his privacy.

I do not have any private messages for Krist. I always felt that he was so close to Kurt and the greatest friend he ever had that a wall would shut if I ever attempted to ask spiritually. The bond between Kurt and Krist just is, and I will forever respect that. It is good to know I can always write him a letter. Expect another one, dude.

Mr. Dave Grohl will like this. I called Johnny to tell him about this cool music video by the Foo Fighters band. The video was 'Learn To Fly,' I cranked that song repeatedly and bought the CD. Best Video Ever. Cocaine Coffee and Cute Girls. He said, you know who Dave Grohl is? I said no. He said he was the drummer from Nirvana. I hope Dave reads this and salutes my coolness as the one person in the world who listened to the Foo Fighters because they were fucking good and not because he was the drummer of Nirvana.

I have a KCGB one-off theory on why Kurt settled on the name Nirvana that is outside the Zen cool name theory. We know Kurt admired what Buzz and Dale were doing with the Melvins. When you say the band's name, you instinctively put a (the) in front of it, but it is just one word, Melvins. There are seven letters in Melvins, and there are seven letters in Nirvana. Secondly, the fourth letter in Melvins and the fourth letter in Nirvana is the letter "V" I think that was Kurt's way of showing respect to Buzz and having confidence in himself to be as good, if not better than Melvins. Either way, I bet Kurt said holy fuck what a great name when he matched seven letters and the V —

When I started this journey, I would use a pen name of Ana V. which would have been short for Ana Vrin, like a narrator with a British accent who was telling the story. In the end, my voice was called upon the stage. Mom sent the message-your eyes are open now. Dave Grohl inspired me to open my eyes, step into the light with no blind faith, and write this memoir with no false hope as if telling me to write for the congregation of people who would know Mary Jo the best, your family, and your friends. I have to say to Dave. Just like you, I was uncomfortable writing about Kurt. Your lyrics shifted my lens when I found a spark of inspiration. What if I wrote this memoir to the congregation of people who knew Kurt best, you and his family and friends? It worked when I thought of his sister Kim, Krist, Buzz, and Dale. Mom told me to trust my gut and run with it, so I did.

Before KCGB, the code name for this book was "Yeah Nudity."

Olivia's Naked Photo

Ms. Burton.

.

Acknowledgments

There are a million resources and people to give credit for influencing the writing of "The Boy From the Porch." This memoir has been told as close to the truth as possible and could not have been accomplished if all involved were unwilling to provide information, dates, times, and memories. My father, Ron, Pops, and Dad read every version and offered corrections and notes every step while Sherry gave the initial thumbs up to the project. "it holds up." As an avid reader and former English teacher, that meant something. Thank you, Pops and Sherry. Marnie Summerfield Smith, for your editorial and ghostwriting guidance from start to finish. I would highly recommend your writing services. The opening chapter has your pen all over it to give credit where credit is due. Need help? Google her name. Brother Tim (Old Timer), for opening up in Arizona and providing some depth to your conversations with Mom. You speak little, but that Excel document was loaded. Who uses Excel as a word processor? Old Timer. Brother Spud took an early belief that the Boy From the Porch was Kurt Cobain and ran with it. I could not use every one of his notes or thoughts because there was debate among brothers on whose memory was the most accurate, but plenty of stories were left to tell between the two. I just left out the disagreements. My sister Joy Scout for giving critical feedback on tone and reverence while offering your perspectives on the story and the love you share with me. Brothers Turk and Balboa were more than open with family stories and interactions with Mom while revisiting her initial visit to them in their dreams— Dr. Fu for editorial review and the glasses of wine. Sorry, I fell down. My bad. A big shout out to Aunty Pat and my cousins for encouragement when reading the initial versions. Aunty is so similar to our Mother. It is an extension of Mom when I meet with her, and I feel it deeply in my heart—so much love for the Robert Mann family.

Writing a memoir eventually takes on a direction of its own. The baseball and whatchamacallit chapters came about well after creating the original outline. Finding the picture of Kurt in 1976 led me back to my friend King (thanks, Gibby), who played on the team. Thank you, King, for providing the copy of the photo and to L. R. Short Collections for permission to use it in the memoir. I do not own the rights to the team picture, but it was published in the Daily World in July 1976. The microfilm needs to be in better shape, which led me to King. Police records, mug shots, and fingerprint cards are considered in the public domain if you know where to look. It was a happy accident when the Buzz Osborne interview about Kurt's initial arrest was published online. Talk about falling in your lap. The other arrest details were outlined in a local publication, "On the Harbor" by John Hughes and Ryan Teague Beckwith, with extensive detail currently left out of most Cobain publications. Good work on Nirvana and other stories surrounding the legacy of Grays Harbor History. Thank you to the Aberdeen Police Department and the Grays Harbor Drug Task Force, who are taking down some serious problems in the community. No disrespect intended with the Whatchamacallit chapter. We were all a part of history.

Several literary references influenced my writing, or I used themes built around something I had read or heard. There was the strategic use of two or three song references meant as recognition to the artist, or if you want to take the spirit route, inspired to write by KCGB's. (Don't Sue Me) Some people might even call them easter eggs with a tribute to Michael Stipe and REM, Buzz Osborne and Dale Crover of the band Melvins, Dave Grohl, and the person who knew Kurt better than anyone, Krist Novoselic. (Miller !!!). The following publications were used as a resource or referenced.

Ron Hulscher — Mom's Eulogy and thousands of conversations.
Everett True — Melody Maker + Nirvana-The Biography.
Krist Novoselic — Of Grunge and Government and the Postcard.
Krist Novoselic — Countless interviews talking about your friend.
Dave Grohl — See above
Dave Grohl — The Storyteller. This is a Call
Charles Cross — Heavier than Heaven.
Jeff Burlingame — Kurt Cobain: Oh Well, Whatever, Nevermind.
John Hughes and Ryan Teague Beckwith — On the Harbor.
Werner Mayr — The Cinderella Tree.
Norman Maclean — A River Runs Through It.
Merril D. Beal — I Will Fight No More Forever - Chief Joseph and the Nez Pierce.
John G. Neihardt — Black Elk Speaks.

Brad Steiger — Indian Medicine Power.

Harper Lee — To Kill a Mockingbird.

Margaret Starbird — The Woman with the Alabaster Jar.

Baigent, Leigh, Lincoln — Holy Blood, Holy Grail

The Boston Globe - Betrayal – The Crisis in the Catholic Church.

Mary Dispenza - Split –A child, a Priest and the Catholic Church.

Shirley Maclaine — What If – A lifetime of questions.

Matthew McConaughey — Greenlights.

The Daily World, Centralia Chronicle

Timberland Regional Library – Aberdeen Branch.

If there were a soundtrack to this memoir, I would start with songs
and albums from these artists. I would have quoted your words if
not for the lawyers, so I quoted your song titles instead.

Charles Hardin Holley – aka Buddy Holly

Simon and Garfunkel: Concert in Central Park

Huey Lewis and the News.

Alan Parsons: Tales of Mystery and Imagination.

REM: Talk About the Passion

REM: Perfect Circle

REM: Supernatural Superserious

Velvet Underground: Pale Blue Eyes

Tom Petty: Damn the Torpedoes

Bob Seger: Hollywood Knights

America: Ventura Highway --- Foo's should cover it.

Foo Fighters: Learn to Fly

Foo Fighters: Congregation - I had serious visions. See next.

Pigeon Feeders: Band in Heaven. Kurt Cobain/River Phoenix

Giants in the Trees: Volume 1 * 2 + 3rd Secret

Butterfly Launches From Spar Pole

(the) Melvins: I Can't Shake It

Melvins: PRICK - Kurt got your message.

Sloan: Twice Removed + entire catalog.

The Brady Kids: Everybody's Smiling * It's a Sunshine Day.

The Vaselines: Jesus wants me for a Sunbeam.

Eric Clapton: Tears in Heaven.

Wishbone Ash

Norah Jones

Boston: More than a feeling.

Nirvana: Teen Spirit

Nirvana: Negative Creep.

Nirvana: Something in the Way

Nirvana: Muddy Banks of the Wishkah side 4 – Tks Krist

Bikini Kill: Riot Grrrl

Sonic Youth: Teenage Riot.

Tony Poukkula: Eruption (High School version – you're old)

Black Ice: The Zoo (Ashleys Pub House version with Don Stone).

Tommila: Last Train (Uncle Joey version)

— Closing Credits

Flock of Seagulls — Praguephilharmonic: Space Age Love Song

Pink Floyd — Wish you were here.

Movies, screenplays, tv, and documentaries are also influences at some point in time when writing. You call upon a scene in your mind, and the words follow. Inspiration can strike at any time and lead you in several directions.

Montage of Heck — Interviews with Cobain Family

Stand By Me — River Phoenix could play any age of Kurt.

The Sandlot. — Baseball, Wendy Peffercorn (Betties)

Forrest Gump. —Turk foot braces -- Gale force winds

St. Elmos's Fire—Plasma Discharge Balboa Dream

The Matrix — Neo and the Oracle. Have a cookie.

Field of Dreams. — If you build it, they will come.

Jaws. — going to need a bigger boat.

Over the Edge — 9th grade Miller Jr High Food Fight

The Hollywood Knights. Newbombs Rule

Pulp Fiction. — Quentin T. Non-linear storytelling.

Booth-to-booth — inspired my outline. Respect.

The Sixth Sense. — Bruce was dead--missed that coming.

National Velvet — Nana Loves You Heather Pi

Pat and Mike — Mom had a little Hepburn in her.

Sister Act — 9 am mass featured the old nun choir

Sound of Music — Nana Loves you, Nic.

Spotlight — Exposure of abuse in the Catholic Church

To Kill a Mockingbird. — Atticus and Scout. Pops and Maria.

The Graduate. — To our neighbor Elinor.

Star Wars Episode 4 — A New Hope - Original Theater Version

In Search of — Star Trek — Leonard Nimoy

Happy Days — Fonzi jumped the shark

Dragnet — Joe Friday – just the facts, mam

X-Files — Spooky Mulder

Saturday Night Live — Things We Did Last Summer

Saturday Night Live — Nirvana, Dave Grohl

Deadwood — Seth Bullock

Photo Credits: We do not intend to infringe on any legitimate intellectual right, artistic rights, or copyright. If you are the rightful owner of any pictures or words posted here and do not want your image or words used in future printings, please contact the publisher. Photos used are courtesy of

The Hulscher Family Archives,
Michael Mann Ancestry Research
The Daily World –> Richard Short –> L. R. Short Collection
Centralia Chronicle — photographer Bob Mackey
Obee Credit Union -> Olympia Tumwater Foundation –>
Licensing-Haus -> Pabst Brewing Company x 2.
My friend King –>Rich's Studio->L. R. Short Collection
Starbucks TM-Logos
Aberdeen Police Department records Public Domain.

Cover Design: Ronaldo Alves – Atmosphere Press

Photo AI enhancements — Fotor.com photo editor

To my friends and family from Aberdeen. Rebuild the Museum and they will come, yes they will come to see the Kurt Cobain Memorial Outhouse.

Please support the 98520 Downtown Aberdeen Music and Art District initiatives.

Endless, Nameless — the Poem

"A mythological Siren screams for food as I reached for a corn dog and thought of the English Channel of expectation when it played out through the explosive end, as if banishing this era into the past and wanting to create my new words and sounds."

Joseph Hulscher

Endless, Nameless is a hidden track at the end of the *Nevermind* Album and is one of the rare Nirvana songs credited to all three members. Vocalist and guitarist Kurt Cobain, bassist Krist Novoselic, and drummer Dave Grohl. The only way to hear it is to let the song *Something in the Way* run out and wait until 13 minutes and 51 seconds have passed on the total run time. It is not credited on the album or included in every copy. The first pressings didn't have it (pissed Kurt off), and many later pressings also left it off. I only found it by accident when I did not change out the CD after the last song played when that 13:51 thing happened, I almost crashed my car because I had turned the volume way up to hear the vocal whispering lyrics to Something in the Way. According to Wiki, this is precisely what the band members had in mind in placing the hidden track. It worked. ~ Wankers.

~*~

That hidden track initially inspired the poem. It was as if Kurt were sitting around eating a corn dog with his friend Krist (the English Channel), discussing the pressures on the band. The explosive end was the hidden track — scared the shit out of me — leaving Kurt free to go in a different direction with his music, either in life or, as it turned out, in death. Kurt was rumored to have an acoustic album in mind post *In Utero*. He was sent a plane ticket with a request from Michael Stipe but never took that flight. The more I thought about it, the more explosive end began to sound like death, so it was after the fact for me when it took on a different meaning. It became darker.

Kurt is the Mythological Siren screaming due to his stomach ailment to open the poem. Dave Grohl reaches for a corndog and thinks about his friend Krist, the English Channel, and the world's expectations of them, post-Kurt Nirvana. They survived on corn dogs early on, thus the reference. The explosive end is the bird shot suicide which leads to banishing this era into the past. A few months later, a depressed Dave found cathartic therapy with refuge in a studio and recorded the first Foo Fighters album by himself, including all vocals and instruments. Krist did his own thing as well, on his terms, and found a quiet place to live in a Murky Slough. I am glad he did. I am so happy he is still here. That is a good thing.

Like in music, the interpretation of the poem is yours to own.

A B E I L N O O U V Y.

2   8 18 19 92   4 18 20   5 92 67 35

67	5	17	1	92	7	14	11	2	69	22	8	73
A	B	C	D	E	F	G	H	I	J	K	L	M

35	18	13	44	6	22	12	20	19	64	33	4	24
N	O	P	Q	R	S	T	U	V	W	X	Y	Z

A Love Letter

www.ingramcontent.com/pod-product-compliance
Lightning Source LLC
Chambersburg PA
CBHW020239130626
46549CB00005B/1969